LETTERS
TO MY
GRANDSONS

ABNEGATION
PUBLISHING

www.abnegationpublishing.com

Paperback ISBN: 979-8-9885422-0-9

Ageless Truth for People of All Ages

LETTERS TO MY GRANDSONS

Mike Andes

To you, my reader, I dedicate this book.
Your future is bright!
… Blessings.

Table of Contents

Introduction

Grandparents are generally considered to be sources of sage advice by those who have them. As for myself, I was the youngest grandchild of both sets of my grandparents, and they all died before I was old enough to learn much from them. So I never got any of that grandparental advice. This book is my attempt to provide that sage advice for my grandchildren: twin seventeen-year-old boys. It is a compilation of letters I wrote to them over a thirteen-month period. They live over a thousand miles away, so my wife and I usually see them only once a year. The idea for the letters was my daughter's, the mother of my grandsons. She asked me to write some stories of my life and some advice for her sons. In the past I have often offered her words of what I would call "wisdom," so this could be considered a compliment!

Grandparents have sage advice because they have lived longer and have experienced more than their grandchildren and their grandchildren's parents. But they must have paid attention and learned from their mistakes for their advice to be worthwhile. Parents who are raising children are typically in their twenties when they start and might be little more than children themselves (I am talking about myself here too) and may lack the wisdom of age, especially if they were not raised well. Since I didn't learn wisdom from my grandparents and learned very little from my parents, I didn't start learning wisdom until I was forty-three years old and divorced. For that reason I didn't teach these things to my own children either. In writing these letters, my hope was to give my grandsons advice that I didn't get so that they will be armed with tools and attitudes that will help them have a better life than I had.

What is missing, it seems, is a pipeline of information from those who have wisdom to those who are getting ready to head out into the world and start making mistakes. I decided to put the letters into a book so that others could possess these ideas and could choose to make improvements in their own life experience. My hope is that these ideas will help people improve their lives, and thereby, the world will be improved. If the world were populated with wise people who love and care for each other, wouldn't that be nice? So the secret is out: at sixty-eight years of age, I have reverted to the idealism of my youth. But I have to give it my best shot!

As I wrote these letters, I intentionally spaced them out with about two weeks between mailings—sometimes it was a little longer due to life happening. The time between the letters allowed my grandsons to read and digest the ideas in each letter before moving on to the next letter. Each idea needs to be considered with some time for thought. The letters in book form could be read in one afternoon, but that would pile on an awful lot, all at once, and the reader would easily lose a lot of it. If you choose to read it all at once, please consider rereading it, one letter at a time, with time for thought in between.

These letters are good for persons of any age. As stated above, I didn't start learning these things until I was forty-three and had "turned over a new leaf" as my mother would say. (The story is in letter 6.) The improvements in my life since have made a miraculous difference for me and my second wife. I wish I had learned these things sooner, but

I am so much better off having learned them when I did, even late, that I can honestly say "It is never too late!" Just like Ebenezer Scrooge in Charles Dickens's *A Christmas Carol*, we are never too old to learn and change.

For me, understanding life is like solving a puzzle with most of the pieces being from the wrong puzzle, and they don't fit anything—not life, not each other. The puzzle pieces are life's experiences and all the various ideas of what is true that are in the world. Oh, and all the pieces start out upside down—they must each be examined carefully, one at a time, and tested for truth. It is my joy and my challenge to figure out which pieces are not part of the true picture and need to be thrown out (false beliefs). If you get rid of the nonsense, the puzzle is easier to solve...but never easy. All the pieces that are true fit together perfectly—with no voids, no imperfections, and no overlaps (contradictions). Slowly a picture begins to take shape.

When completed, the picture is of *perfect knowledge*. Most people will say that completing the puzzle is impossible...why even try? But that just makes me want to keep going. Most people are following false beliefs anyway; why should I let them distract me? I might not finish the puzzle, but I can get it started for other people to come along after me and finish later. The only way for me to fail is to not share what I have learned. I must share with the world what pieces have proven themselves to be true and how they fit together in mutual support to create a beautiful picture of what makes life worth living. That is why I wrote this book, *Letters to My Grandsons*. When I get it published, failure is impossible because the ideas will be out there, waiting to be found by those who are looking. One thing is for sure, since beginning my quest for truth, life has never been boring!

Who am I to give advice? I am a seeker of truth. I am not an academic. I do not have letters after my name or "Dr." before it; I don't even have a bachelor's degree. But I am inquisitive. As a child I was the one always asking "Why?" And, yes, my parents usually answered with "Because I said so!" I hope that, like me, you have an inquisitive mind, one that is not satisfied with contrived answers and dubious belief systems. I am also strongly independent; my parents saw it as rebellious (and they were not wrong), but my motto has always been: "Do not follow the crowd!" (Unless, by some strange coincidence, they happen to be going in the correct direction.) I think for myself, always questioning what I am being told. I hope that you do not desire to be spoon-fed and follow the crowd but, instead, yearn for understanding, for truth. I hope that you, too, ask "Why?"

In college I studied engineering because my father wanted me to. (This story is in letter 1.) I did not earn my degree, but I did complete all the requirements for graduation except for earning a 2.0 GPA. ("A good time was had by all!") When I did make it to class, I learned that, in science and engineering classes, there were often associated lab classes in which we were able to prove the laws we were taught in the classroom and thus *know* that the laws were true because they worked in practice. Engineering is all about the practical application of scientific law. I learned how to analyze a situation, gather the necessary data, and, by using some imagination and the proper scientific laws, create a solution—I learned how to problem solve, to think logically and critically...and to *test* everything!

With that scientific methodology in mind, I have applied the same approach to the experience of life: What if there are laws that make sense of life? What if there are laws that if we can discover them, much as Isaac Newton discovered the basic laws of physics, we can use them to improve the quality of the lives of all those who *choose* to live by them? I have been searching for these laws since I was a teenager, with some success, and discovered some big truths in 1998, but I have made better progress since 2006 when I discovered *personal responsibility*; thank you, Dave Ramsey! How I discovered these laws and truths and what I have discovered since applying them to my life are the subject of these letters I wrote to my grandsons. But I hope I haven't done too much of the work, because there is great value in the exercise of seeking and discovering. I do not expect my grandsons, or you, to believe whatever I write without thinking about it and examining it through experimentation. *Let the world be your laboratory!*

As you read this book and then, for the rest of your life, approach life as a big laboratory experiment, always discovering new truths. Keep your mind wide open, and do not accept what you are told without testing it for yourself. What an adventure life becomes! You are always engaged in an experiment; problems, instead of being overwhelming, become challenges; learning is lifelong. The result is a high-quality life of intention and purpose. It is never boring; that's for sure!

Enjoy the adventure! I hope to hear from you—we can compare notes!

Letter 1: Freedom!

Your life is yours to do with as you wish.

Dear Eddy and Alan,

This is your Grandpa Andes writing. Your mom asked me to write some letters with advice and family stories for you guys. I believe that it is her hope that you can get to know me and my parents better and learn some of the lessons I have learned from my experiences in my sixty-six years of life. It is a great idea with which I am very happy to comply. These letters will be short, so hopefully they will not be tiresome. I'll try to mail one every few weeks. I hope you guys will find these letters of advice and stories of life interesting.

Of note, I have learned the most about life from making errors and suffering the consequences of those errors. With these letters you have the opportunity to learn from my mistakes, so you don't have to suffer like I did. Before you make a decision, think about the long-term probable outcomes of the various options. You will make better choices...and suffer less.

But you will make mistakes anyway. When you do make a mistake, own up to it. Apologize and make amends to anyone you may have hurt—decide to never do that again.

Be a person that you can be proud of!

You can be smart about life...or not.

Smart people think about their life as if they had total control of it. Now, things happen that a person cannot control, so no one has *total* control of their life. But if you set goals for yourself, create a plan for achieving those goals, and then go to work and work, work, work, you will have a life of achievement. You will be a difference maker, but the big difference is that your life will have a lasting *positive* impact on the world at large.

The other way of doing life—the way most people do it—is to not plan at all. They don't even decide to not plan. They just take life as it comes, set no goals, make decisions based on how they feel at the moment, and end up who knows where. Dave Ramsey's website says that 78 percent of Americans are living paycheck to paycheck,[1] having no savings and no plan for retirement. They end up being a drain on society and on their families...and are very unfulfilled in the process.

Truth

Your life is yours to do with as you wish. The choice is yours. You are the only person that has the power to decide what to do with your life. This is a great opportunity, and you guys are at a time in your lives where the choices you make now can affect you for the rest of your life. So this is important!

True Story

When I was a senior in high school, I took a class called Architectural Drawing. I loved it! I decided I wanted to become an architect, and I told my father. He said to me, "You don't want to be an architect; architects are stupid! You want to be an engineer." He was a builder and had experienced problems with building plans that had errors; he told me some of them. Since I admired my father and wanted to please him, I enrolled in the School of Engineering at the University of Kansas. I never finished my degree because I wasn't interested in engineering. I have regretted both of those decisions—to not study architecture and to not finish my degree—my whole life.

Do not do something simply because someone tells you to do it—especially when it will affect your life. Recognize the fact that no one can live your life for you. You, and you alone, have the right and the power to choose how you are going to live your life. Do not hesitate to ask for advice, but you do not have to take it. That includes the advice I am giving you in these letters.

Think

Take time to be alone with your phone off and no distractions for at least twenty minutes at a time every day for a week. Spend this time thinking about your life:

- What kind of career do I want?
- What kind of family do I want?
- Where do I want to live?
- Who do I want to be? What kind of personality traits do I want to have? This is a big question, and it will be explored in a future letter: "Who Do You Want to Be?"

- Think of other areas of life to consider.
- In every area of life, think about people who you believe are doing that area of life well and look at what works for them and consider if it would work for you.
- Be practical—what works? Don't make it your goal to be the king of England or a similar impossibility because it cannot happen. But still, *think big!*
- *You can do whatever you set your mind to if you are willing to do the work necessary to make it happen.*

By the way, this exercise of taking time every day alone in thought is a good habit to start.

I would be interested in hearing what you are thinking about. Give me a call or an email with your thoughts.

With love,
Grandpa

Remember

Achievement is not easy, but it is highly satisfying.

1. Set goals.
2. Create plans to accomplish those goals.
3. Go to work and work, work, work to make it happen.
4. Don't forget to have fun too! But do your work first.

Letter 2: Personal Responsibility

With freedom comes responsibility.

Dear Alan and Eddy,

Personal responsibility is one of the most powerful truths there is. That is why I chose to make it the subject of the second letter, because it needs to be understood before other truths are useful.

Truth

With freedom comes responsibility. In the first letter, we talked about freedom, but now comes the other side of the same coin: responsibility. Having the freedom to choose what we want to do with our lives is an incredible opportunity. It is also a large responsibility because if we accept the liberating idea that we are in control of our life, we then cannot blame our bad choices, failures, or shortcomings on circumstances or other people. We must be accountable. In life everything has a cost it seems, and the cost of freedom is accountability. You can't have one without the other!

True Story

The day I turned sixteen, in 1971, was the most anticipated day of my life up to then. The first thing I wanted to do that day was to get my driver's license! My dad let me go to school late, and he drove me to the driver's license bureau to be tested. I passed on the first try! My dad let me drive to school with him as a passenger! What a great feeling of growing up! It was a huge milestone of adult freedom. Now I could go where I wanted when I wanted!

A few days later, I wanted to take a drive by myself for the first time. I asked my dad if I could borrow his car. He didn't say anything; he just reached into his pocket and pulled out his car keys, and I put out my hand, palm up, for him to drop them into it. He dangled the keys in the air for a few seconds but did not drop them until I looked him in the eye. When he knew that he had my attention, he said something: "Remember, Mike; with freedom comes responsibility!" I'll never forget that. I understood right away that with adult-sized freedom comes adult-sized responsibility.

As the driver of a car, you are responsible for the safety of yourself, of other people in the car, and of every other person in the vicinity. *Don't ever forget that!*

As the years have gone by I have come to understand, that in every situation, in all of life: with freedom comes responsibility. The inverse is also true: if I want more freedom, I must take on more responsibility. This means that taking on responsibility is a very liberating act! Instead of a sobering and possibly frightening idea, responsibility is an exciting and empowering idea. Think of the possibilities!

Most people want to avoid responsibility because they want to just get by—they want to escape as much accountability as possible. To do that, they push responsibility off onto others and blame others if possible. Trying to avoid responsibility is a guarantee of having a miserable life. I was one of those people too. You will never have self-respect if you do that, and I didn't. You don't want to go there.

If you choose to not take responsibility, then you become a victim because you are giving somebody else the right to make your choices for you, and you must take whatever you get!

Instead, take responsibility for everything you have within your control. Start with small things and work up to bigger things. You already have some responsibilities, I am sure, like keeping your room clean, taking care of your pets, etc. Make sure you are diligent and take care of your responsibilities without being told, and you will gain the trust of your parents. As trust is built, they will feel like you will be able to handle more freedom. If you are given more freedom, do not be tempted to abuse that freedom, or you will lose their trust and lose those freedoms. This is the way life works in the adult world as well. When you do your work well, without being told, you will be given more responsibilities (like a promotion) and more pay. Work will be the subject of a future letter.

Responsibilities of every person:

1. *Make sure you and your family are taken care of*—that is your first responsibility.
2. *Do all you can do to alleviate the problems of the world.* As a citizen of the world, it is your responsibility to help those who need help to the extent that you are able. Be careful; there is a right way to help and a wrong way. This is a long story and will be covered in

a future letter but, briefly, don't just throw money at the problem. Money by itself solves nothing in the long term—it creates dependency. Give your time, over a period, establish relationships and trust, and require accountability. Then lasting change for the better can happen.

3. *Don't worry about things outside of your control.* Don't allow yourself to be burdened by things people cannot control. For example, you cannot stop earthquakes or tornadoes, but you can design and build structures that withstand their destructive forces. (See! I should have been an architect! Ha ha!)

4. *Who you are is your responsibility!* Is it possible to change who you are? It is more than a possibility; it is your *responsibility* to change yourself into a loving, compassionate human. We are all born into life only caring about our own needs. Babies only know what they want: food, rest, holding, diapers changed, etc. It is months before they start to realize that there are other people in the world, and the journey of change begins—a change from perfectly selfish to something less selfish. If the baby has good parents, it will be taught to consider other people to be equally important to itself. This is a huge challenge, and I am still working on me and probably will be for the rest of my life. But the truth is that to be caring for other people is the road to happiness: you will have better relationships, and relationships are where happiness is found. The opposite of that—to care only about yourself—is the road to misery. It is a lonely and unhappy life. Choose to be loving. Be a person that you can be proud of—a person who is loving and considerate and compassionate. More on this in a future letter: "Who Do You Want to Be?"

Think

Take time to be alone with your phone off and no distractions for at least twenty minutes at a time every day for a week. Spend this time thinking and ask yourself:

1. *Is there a relationship between freedom and responsibility?* If I refuse to take care of my responsibilities, will I lose freedom? Or if I take care of my responsibilities well and accept additional responsibilities, will I gain freedom?

2. *Do I want to be a responsible person?* What would be the advantages and disadvantages?

3. *Or do I want to be an irresponsible person?* What would be the advantages and disadvantages? How do I feel about myself if I choose to be irresponsible?

A final thought: How can these letters be of value to you? Having knowledge by itself is of limited value. For knowledge to have value, it must be applied to your life. You must use truth in your life by living it; then it will generate value for you. Knowledge put into action is wisdom.

Experiment. Test these ideas to see if they are true—apply one to your life and see if it works!

With love,
Grandpa

Letter 3: Education

Decide what you want to do in life, then determine what education may be needed to give yourself a head start.

Dear Eddy and Alan,

This subject is less deep than the others have been thus far. It is mostly practical information and is something we have talked about a little bit. But it is a very important conversation we need to have now because, in a couple of years, you will be graduating from high school, and you will need to have a plan for what you want to do after that. Basically you should expect to go to work, or continue your education, or some of both. If you have a career path you wish to pursue, it will probably require some sort of education.

Have you talked to your parents about their expectations of you after high school? The direction you choose is up to you, but they will probably not want to have you guys living with them until you are thirty! Most parents are good with children living in their house if they are in school or trade school full time, and there is usually a "grace period" (probably less than six months) for saving some money so you can get a place of your own. This is a conversation that you need to think about, prepare for, and initiate with your parents. It is part of preparing for and becoming an adult.

In letter 1, I gave you guys some things to consider about your life:

- What kind of career do I want?
- Where do I want to live?
- *You can do whatever you set your mind to if you are willing to do the work necessary to make it happen.*

Did you think about these things? Your whole life is in front of you. Where would you like to go? What would you like to do with it? *Dream big!*

Assignment

Make plans for a potential career path. What work would you like to do for the next forty-five years (including school) if you're like most people (Plan A)? Or what work would you like to do for the next twenty-five to thirty years if you live well below your income and save money aggressively (Plan B)? I would recommend Plan B.

Whichever it is, you need to decide now what you want to do after high school. If you want to go to college for a science or engineering degree, it's a little late to get the math you will need for that if you haven't taken algebra and geometry—you can get the extra math in college, but it is free in high school. You may have already done this, but if not, now is the time.

Consider, too, the practical side of your dream:

1. How long will it take you to get the education you will need to pursue your dream?

2. How much will your education cost? And how can you get a good education with the least expense? There are practical ways for achieving the goal of a good education. (See ROI below.)

3. How will you pay for your education? Your grandma and I have a small scholarship fund for both of you to share. It will help, but it may not be enough to get you the education that you want. So we need to work on a plan on how to accomplish your goals. I am pretty good at finances, so I am glad to help with planning—just let me know. I would love to help!

What if you don't have an idea for a career path? No problem! You do not have to go to college or trade school right out of high school. Get a job in a field you think might be interesting but that you're not sure about, and rent an inexpensive place to live, with roommates to help you pay the rent and utilities (make sure they are trustworthy). Save money from your job while you are looking for a career that you enjoy. More about money in a future letter.

While you are not settled on a career path, and while you are in school, do not take on long-term responsibilities like getting married or buying a house, and *never* borrow money or use credit! Try to plan on not marrying until you are out of school or at least in your last year of college. Marriage is the subject of a future letter.

Return on Investment (ROI) for College

Higher education is expensive. You will be investing a lot of money and a lot of time. Make sure it is worth what you are paying.

- *Choice of degree:* Don't pay $100,000 for a degree that has no value to an employer—you will have wasted your money. Choose a degree that there is a demand for in the marketplace as well as one you are interested in. For example, if you want to be an artist and get a degree in art, you will have a very difficult time trying to earn a living as an artist right out of school. There are a few places that hire artists, like Hallmark Cards in Kansas City or an advertising agency in a large metropolitan city. If you want to be a freelance artist (to work for yourself), you will need to support yourself for a while, doing something else as you develop your craft and build a following—that takes time.

- *Choice of college:* Don't go to an expensive private college when you can get the same degree at a state college, because it is very rare that an employer cares where you got your degree. (If a prospective employer wants you to have a degree from a prestigious school, you will need to decide if you want to work for someone that petty.) The important thing is did you learn anything? So your grades *are* important.

- *The first two years* can be done inexpensively at a community college while you're living at home. Make sure the classes you take will transfer to the college you'll eventually get your degree from and that the classes are applicable to the degree you are working toward. So talk to the college you wish to graduate from first before enrolling at a community college.

- *Work at a job* while you are in college to pay for it. During your summer break, work at several jobs part time or one really good job and save the money to support yourself during the school year.

- *Get good grades now!* If you want to drastically reduce your out-of-pocket expenses for college, or possibly have zero college expenses, get good grades in high school! With a good academic record in high school, you will be eligible for grants (monetary gifts from the government, schools, and organizations to pay for school) and scholarships (private grants). These grants and scholarships are *free money* that you do not have to repay! But you must keep your grades up for your entire college career—you want to do that anyway because employers do look at your grades. Plan to apply for fifty grants and/or scholarships each year of college.
- *Do not borrow money for school…or anything else!* If the first thing you do right out of high school is go into debt, you will be putting yourself in a financial hole and putting *a lot* of stress on yourself. That is a bigger problem than you can know right now. That is a really bad idea! Life is hard enough without the financial burden of a student loan…or debt of any kind! Most college graduates have student loans of tens of thousands of dollars with monthly payments of several hundred dollars, and it takes ten years or more to pay them off!
- *Be smart!* Plan ahead and create a method of paying for school as you go. *Debt Free Degree* by Anthony ONeal[2] is a book that explains all this and more. If one of you would like to have a copy, let me know and I will send it to you.

With love,
Grandpa

Letter 4: Think

Never surrender your thinking to someone else.

Dear Alan and Eddy,

This letter is fairly brief. It consists of mainly a true story of my boy-hood that led me to a moment of truth in my life and has made a profound impact on how I think and approach life. This letter contains just one thought, a very simple thought but a very important thought:

Do not *follow the crowd! They don't know where they are going!*

True Story

When I was a boy of around ten to twelve years of age, I had a bunch of friends in the neighborhood whom I hung around with. We must have been bored one afternoon when someone suggested that we should go TP the Rogers' house. (Not their real name.) The Rogers boys were two brothers who were not to our liking because they didn't play sports like we did. It was a stupid and mean thing to do, but you know how a bunch of boys think—they don't! Here's how little we were thinking: It was daylight, for Pete's sake! So we all went to our respective houses and got eggs and toilet paper, met back at the Rogers' house, and proceeded to TP and throw eggs at the house. When the eggs ran out, someone picked up a walnut and threw that, and then someone threw a walnut through a window. (I hope it was an accident, but I don't know.) We all scattered after that.

Well, guess what? We had been seen by a neighbor, who called all our parents. My dad said to me, "Mike, I need to see you in the garage right now!" This usually meant a whipping, so I knew I was in big trouble. After telling me that he knew what we did, he asked me, "Why did you do that?" I said, "Everyone else was doing it!" He said, "Would you follow them over a cliff?!" followed by this statement, which was one I will never forget, *"Never surrender your thinking to someone else!"*

Those words seared themselves right into my brain with incredible clarity and absolute truth. They spoke to my desire to be independent and self-directed. I have always had a strong independent will, but those words made *sense* of my willfulness because of their undeniable logic.

Think about what you are doing and why you are doing it. Is it working for you? If not, figure out a better way. Do not follow the crowd. They don't know where they are going. In letter 1, I wrote that Dave Ramsey's website says that 78 percent of Americans are living paycheck to paycheck[1], having no savings and no plan for retirement. That is almost eight out of ten people—adults—who have no plan…and don't care. Do not follow them! They are lost! Instead figure out how to do life better, make your life better, then teach other people *who want to learn.*

Carefully consider what you read, even in a classroom. For example, I am currently taking a college class online in philosophy. One of the videos I was assigned to watch as part of my homework contained a statement that was illogical. Because I have made my own private study of what is true for many years, I knew that the statement was wrong. One of my classmates, who is probably around twenty years old, made the comment in her paper that the statement made no sense, and I responded that she was right. She is the exception—she is an independent thinker. We need more people like her!

Analyze the information you receive. For example, I was watching a local TV news broadcast about a week ago, and there was a national news story about how scientists had discovered that we were "living in the past" because our senses were giving us information that was *fifteen seconds old!* How many people watching that newscast thought about what was being told to them? You could not play sports, you could not drive a car, you could not do almost anything if this story was true. Yet I am willing to bet that most people heard it and believed it without thinking about it. What did the scientists really discover? Who knows. Was it a test to see if anyone was paying attention? Maybe. My point is that there is a lot of garbage circulating around out there (most of what you see and hear). Think about what you see and hear before believing it.

Lastly, carefully consider what I am writing in these letters. Does what you are reading make sense? If you were to apply my ideas to your life, would you expect to get a good result or not? Do not take my word for anything without first thinking about it and then testing it.

What should you believe? What is the truth? That is the subject of my next letter!

Remember this truth from your great-grandfather: "Never surrender your thinking to someone else."

With love,
Grandpa

Letter 5: Truth

How do you separate fact from fiction?

Dear Eddy and Alan,

I can preach all day long, but what do my words mean to you? How can you, Eddy and Alan, come to *know* what is true? What I am about to tell you I have never read or heard. It is the result of many years of my personal experience, thought, and testing.

There are two kinds of truth:

1. *The truth society tells you.* This is not truth at all but rather false beliefs that appeal to our natural tendency to be selfish. Since we have that tendency, we might accept what society tells us is true without thinking about it. For example, saying "Having a lot of money will make me happy because I don't want to have to work. I can just have fun and not worry about how to pay for all the fun I am

having." This sounds very appealing, doesn't it? Even as I write this, it sounds appealing to me, even though I know it is not true. I lived this way for many years! It is false because money does not make a person happy. There are lots of miserable rich people, so having a lot of money does not guarantee happiness. And there are lots of happy poor people, so being poor does not guarantee misery.

2. *The real Truth.* This is the stuff that makes a person not only happy but also joyous and fulfilled. For example, helping people who need help is what brings a person joy. This is True. I know this to be True because I have spent a lot of years doing volunteer work, helping people who need help, and it is by far the most joyful thing I have done with my time. Happiness is superficial and short term. Joy is a deep satisfaction and is long lasting.

I distinguish between "truth" (#1 above) and "Truth" (#2 above) with capitalization. What the world would have you believe is truth. What is not obvious but is actually true I call Truth.

The Truth about Truth: *the way to know that something is True is to test it.*

If you do not test your beliefs, you will never know if they are true; they will only be beliefs. What if what you have been told is not true? If you don't test what others tell you, you will not know whether to accept it as truth or not—you could easily be following a false belief. Since it is a natural tendency of people to follow their selfish desires, and most people do not even think about life and how it works (letter 1), most people *are* following false beliefs. Don't be one of them (letter 4)!

How does a person test an idea for Truth? Apply it to your life. Give it some time—a few months at least, maybe a year or more. See if your life is improved because of this new practice. Also, something cannot be Truth if it benefits you but harms someone else. So as part of gauging if something is causing improvement in your life, make sure it meets two requirements:

1. *It must be good for you and for everyone else.* To be bad for others there must be real damage and not just making someone uncomfortable. For example, if I decide to be honest and stop pretending that someone's rude behavior is not a problem for me, that person is going to have hurt feelings if I don't want to be around them anymore. (Of course I tell them I have made that decision and why.) But their hurt feelings are a result of me no longer enabling their bad behavior and should not keep me from doing the right thing. By not associating with someone who is rude to me, I may have lost a friend (if they were a friend to begin with), but I will be gaining a lot of self-respect by not allowing myself to be abused anymore. Besides, maybe my decision to distance myself from them could cause them to rethink how they treat people, which would be a good thing for them!

2. *The good effects must be good in the short term and in the long term— across the years.*[3]

Is Truth the same for everyone? Yes! Of course most people do not bother themselves with questions like "What is truth?" So they have probably not tested ideas to see if they are true. If it sounds good, or if all their friends believe it, that's good enough for them! So their idea of what truth is should not be any concern for you. Remember, *you must think for yourself!* Yes, if an idea has a good result for you and for everyone over the short and long term, it is universally True—*even if no one agrees with you.* Be prepared for that to happen, I can tell you!

Truth is not easy to find, but I have done some of the work for you. Here are some examples in a table below of what I believe to be Truth. But do not take my word for it! For Truth to be true for you, *you must test it for yourself!* This is an extremely important part!

Examples of things that don't work:	Examples of things that do work:
Being selfish: living as if getting what you want is the only thing that matters. You might get what you want, but it won't make you happy.	Being in-service to others gives tremendous satisfaction. It's the best feeling in the world. Try it. You'll like it!
Believing that things (stuff) will make you happy: big house, money, cars, vacations…These things are not bad, but they cannot make you happy long term.	Relationships are what life is all about: treating others as you wish others would treat you makes for good relationships, which makes for a great life.
Believing that life has been planned for you and that your destiny is set—your job is to let it happen. The Truth is that the choices you make must be consistent and part of a plan or you will go nowhere.	Exercise your freedom: be self-directed. Setting goals and working hard to reach them is very fulfilling. Reach for the stars!

Examples of things that don't work:	Examples of things that do work:
Letting the influence of advertising be an excuse for buying things you cannot afford, using credit. You will be broke and in debt; that is a miserable and frightening place to be (personal experience).	Budget your money; spend much less than you earn; save for a rainy day and for big purchases; never use credit. Assume that God owns everything, and you are just His steward. You will have financial stability.
Overeating, not exercising, putting foreign substances in your body like drugs, alcohol, tobacco. If you are not taking care of your body, you will certainly be physically miserable.	Eat lots of vegetables, exercise daily, and get a good night's sleep. You will be sick less and live longer—and you will have more energy and feel better in the process.
Trying to take shortcuts to get what you want. You cannot have self-respect if you do this.	Honesty is the best policy— expect to *earn* everything you get in life. What you *deserve* is what you *earn!*

Examples of things that don't work:	Examples of things that do work:
Dodging responsibility—do not avoid that which is your responsibility by letting others make your decisions for you. You will have to take whatever they give you, and you will be a victim.	Your life is yours to do with as you wish (letter 1). This is both a great *freedom* and a great *responsibility*. Accepting responsibility is what gives you freedom (letter 2).
Believing you are a bad person. Unfortunately some religions are responsible for spreading this lie. Don't believe it! If you don't feel worthy, how can you have good relationships?	Believe in yourself: only if you feel worthy will you allow yourself to try to succeed. You can do whatever you set your mind to if you are willing to do the work necessary to make it happen (letter 1).
Wanting life to be easy: no problems, just fun! But an easy life soon becomes a boring life, and fun is good, but it is not the main thing.	It is the challenges in life that make it interesting—and overcoming them that make it rewarding.

Examples of things that don't work:	Examples of things that do work:
Believing that "I am who I am, and nothing can change that." (I used to say these words myself, I am very sorry to say.)	You can be the person you want to be. But to change who you are takes clear vision, determination, and *hard work!* No one can do this for you, by the way

This is just a small sample. Look for Truth for yourself. You will find it. *Do not take my word for it!* Test these things and see if they are True! Then live your truths for a great life.

Truth is older than the universe. There are laws that have been discovered by scientists and mathematicians that control how the universe functions. Gravity is a great example; it controls the physical interaction of the planets and galaxies as well as the interaction of molecular-sized particles. These interactions are predictable; they have been modeled with mathematical formulas, and they are *perfectly consistent in every case.*

Chemistry is the science of the interaction of different chemicals in the world—certain chemicals will react in exactly the same way with other certain chemicals when under identical circumstances, *perfectly consistent in every case.*

Scientists and mathematicians are studying the universe and are learning about how it works and how it came into being. Without these laws that they have discovered, the universe could not have come into being. Therefore, these laws are older than the universe; they were operating before the universe came into being, long before they were discovered by humans.

Here's what I'm getting to: I believe that Truth is like the laws of science. It is universal—it works the same way for everyone, and it is perfectly consistent—it works every time. It is also difficult to discover. Truth works whether we are paying attention to it or even have knowledge of it. It, too, has been operating far longer than anyone has been aware of it, and people are discovering more about it all the time—or at least those who are looking for it...and have an open mind to accept it.

The belief that there is such a thing as Truth is, at this time in history, not popular. Most of the people you talk to, if they have an opinion about truth, will tell you that because every person has a different experience, their beliefs are different. Therefore, truth is relative, meaning that truth is variable—it is dependent upon the experience and beliefs of the individual. Don't believe them! They are mixing up "belief" with "truth." Prove for yourself what is true, and the opinions of other people will not lead you astray. Listen to what others say but weigh it against what you have tested and proven to yourself to be true to determine if it might have validity and value. Do *not* claim anything to be true if you have not tested it and are not using it in your life with good results.

Testing for Truth also means that you will be living your truth. When you find that an idea you are testing in your life has good results, you will want to keep using it, and you will be living your Truth. On the other hand, when you find that an idea you are testing in your life has bad results, you will want to reject that falsehood and not keep getting bad results. You must be observant in this process. Mistakes will still be made, but if you are constantly vigilant, you will see where you have made a mistake, and then you can adjust your theory and then test the new theory.

The result of all this searching for Truth, testing for Truth, and living out your Truths is that you will have a life that is in harmony with what *truly* results in a good outcome and rejecting what results in a bad outcome. You will have a life that is in accord with the universe, living a life of intention and purpose, in harmony with nature and your fellow humans. Sounds ideal, doesn't it? In a future letter, we will look at Utopia, "a place of ideal perfection especially in laws, government, and social conditions."[4] Things will really get interesting then!

One more thing about Truth: if you have tested for Truth and are continuing to apply what you have found to be true to your life, you will *know* what is true from your own experience. The benefit is that when a new idea comes along which you can see conflicts with Truth, you will not be caught up in the fever of "I've got to be up to date!" or "I don't want to miss out!" You will not be lured into a fad, or worse a fraud, that is foolish by its very nature. Even better, when bad times come—and they will come—you will not be in despair or panic; you will be standing on firm ground.

This is a *lot* to digest. These are probably brand-new ideas that you guys may have never considered, so it may take a lot of thought and many rereadings before it starts to make sense. It is, nevertheless, of great importance. Please take your time and consider it carefully.

With love,
Grandpa

How Do We Find Truth?

This is a paper I wrote for my own interest while taking a class in philosophy last year. It was not part of my letter to my grandsons because the letter was already extralong.

In the world of science, the empirical method has been used for hundreds of years with great success in discovering the truth about the world we live in. I am going from memory of science classes taken almost fifty years ago. Here it is:

1. The scientist observes a particular phenomenon, which arouses a question: "Why does *that* happen?"
2. Preliminary testing may narrow down the possibilities as to the causes, and some potential answers may emerge.
3. Each of these potential answers becomes a hypothesis: "[*That*] happens because of [*this*]."
4. The scientist attempts to create an experiment in a controlled environment where the variables can be limited to just one: the hypothetical. Each hypothesis must be tested in a separate experiment. (We were warned by our science teachers to be careful not to let our hypotheses cloud our observations—record exactly what we observed and *keep an open mind!*)
5. By making observations during the experiments, recording those observations, and then analyzing the data, the scientist attempts to answer the question raised in Step 1 above.

When scientists began using this method, scientific discovery made massive steps forward.

This method is how we can test for Truth, Truth that we can apply to our lives. My wife and I started doing this about twenty years ago and have been doing it ever since. This is how I came to discover what I am writing about in these letters. (Our first experiment was: "Can one person make a difference in the workplace?" The answer is "Yes! But it takes time—a few months." Try it. It's fun.)

My search for Truth is not complete by any means! These letters encompass a lot of life but are not the last word! There is a universe of Truth out there that is yet undiscovered, so my search continues… probably for the rest of my life.

I invite you to join me and test for Truth in your own life. Will you discover that what I hold to be true will be true for you as well? I believe so. As I stated in the letter, Truth is universal: true for everyone, every time, in every situation. But do not prejudge based on your hypothesis.

This is *not* a popular thought these days, but when I was young, there was a thing called "common sense." It was truths that were obvious to almost everyone (*common*), and these truths could be lived out in your life with a good result (they made *sense*). Things like "Come in out of the rain" and "Don't play in the street." Nowadays people want you to believe that everyone's truth is different, so there is no such thing as truth. Don't believe them—again, they are confusing "truth" with "belief." Test for truth for yourself!

April 24, 2022

Letter 6: Honesty

Honesty is the best policy.

Dear Alan and Eddy,

It has been two months since I wrote a letter. I got very busy with school, and I got sick from coronavirus. So this letter is overdue. I'm sorry. I hope you guys are well and doing well in school. Have you thought about what I have written so far? Have you gotten anything out of it? I would love to hear from you.

Let's get started. Before anything else, you must know this: Honesty *does* have to do with how you interact with other people and with treating them as you would like to be treated. But more importantly, it has to do with how you feel about yourself. *You must have self-respect*, but if you are dishonest, you cannot have self-respect. Self-respect is the subject of my next letter.

Honesty is far more than following the rules and staying out of jail. It is the minimum requirement for and the foundation upon which you build your self-respect. The more honest you are, the stronger your foundation of self-respect. If you don't have self-respect, you have nothing. And it all starts with honesty.

There are two types of honesty:

1. *Honesty with others.* This is critical if you are to ever have trusting and trusted friends. Having good friends that you can depend on and who can depend on you is important in having a good life. "Relationships" is the title of a future letter.
2. *Honesty with yourself.* This is the tough one and the even more important one. We'll get to it in the second half of this letter.

True Story

Like my mother I project my honesty onto the people around me. In other words, since I am honest, I just assume everyone else is honest as well. My dad used to make fun of her, saying she had rose-colored glasses. But when, as a small child, I recognized this difference between my parents, I made an intentional decision: I decided that I wanted to give people the benefit of the doubt and assume that they are trustworthy. I would rather be trusting than cynical. But if it's important, I get it in writing! "Trust but verify!"—an old Russian expression.

In 1986 (I was thirty-one) I got into business with a man I trusted. As you may guess, this man I got into business with was *not* trustworthy; in fact, he stole a large sum of money from me. Eventually he paid it back, but our partnership was over. Many years later, about ten years ago, I did some work for him, but knowing what kind of person he used to be, I didn't trust him too far. But I hoped that he had learned in the twenty-six years since we had been partners that honesty was the best policy. He hadn't! He ended up stealing a few hundred dollars from me, and I stopped doing work for him. But I felt sorry for him. For a small amount of money, he was willing, once again, to destroy his self-respect and destroy our relationship. He died not long ago and went to his grave without ever having a good opinion of himself, but he didn't even know it. (You can know things and not know them consciously. This comes under "Honesty with yourself" below.) How sad is that?! *Don't be that guy!* Guard your self-respect with untiring zeal by being fanatically honest!

Note

If you haven't noticed yet, everything is tied to everything else. There is (hopefully) total unity in my system of belief—each belief supports the others with no contradictions. This is one reason I believe these things to be Truth. If you find contradictions, you have found falsehood. If you get the feeling that something smells fishy, pay attention to that feeling!

Honesty in Friendships

You want to have a reputation for honesty. Here's why: If you discover that someone has not been honest with you, how does that make you feel? Not good, right? When someone is dishonest with you, they are telling you that they do not respect you or value your friendship. It is something you need to confront right away. Talk to them; give them the opportunity to make it right and repair the loss of trust. If they choose not to confess or make amends, they are not your friend. Let them know that if they want to repair the friendship, you are open to that idea. But it will take a long time before you can fully trust them again. If you have a bad reputation, people will not trust you, and they will not want to be friends.

Truth

Trust is difficult to earn but easy to lose.

Honesty in Business

Dave Ramsey recently wrote a book titled *Baby Steps Millionaires*.[5] He interviewed thousands of people who had a net worth of $1,000,000 or more. He found that the most common characteristic was honesty. Not just honesty but fanatical honesty. And not just common but *100 percent of millionaires claimed to be fanatically honest*. It makes sense. If you are dishonest, your customers won't keep coming back, and your suppliers won't want to sell to you either. The dishonest man I told you about above? He was never successful in business either.

When you have a job working for someone, be honest above everything else. Dishonesty in the workplace will get you fired immediately and potentially prosecuted. But honesty in the workplace is much more than not stealing or lying. It is arriving early, staying late, *working hard* to *earn* your pay, and giving your employer more than they expect. If you are the hardest worker and the most reliable, you will be a highly valued employee and will likely be rewarded. You will also go home after work satisfied that you have done your best.

Honesty with Yourself

This is not as easy as it sounds.

Truth

From a Hallmark movie I saw during this past Christmas season: "You must be honest with yourself and with other people or you will have no peace." (I don't remember the name of the movie.) I believe that honesty with yourself is more important but the most difficult. Being honest with yourself requires a person to look at themselves critically—looking in an objective way as if you were looking at yourself from a distance, apart from yourself. Whom do you see?

In a twelve-step program, it is step four—a fearless moral inventory. You need to look at the good, the bad, and the ugly. Write it all down. Own it. Once the moral inventory is completed and written down, start improving on your good points and changing your bad behaviors to good ones. It sounds hard...and it is! But the alternative is to remain who you are; remember my True Story above. Be open to self-improvement, for it is the best thing you can do in this life! Being honest with yourself is where it starts. I will write in more detail about this process in a future letter: "Who Do You Want to Be?"

A Sad but True Story

When I was married to my first wife, your nanna, she tried many, many times to get me to change. I was a spoiled, immature, and insecure jerk who had zero self-respect. I was sober, honest, faithful, and hardworking, but that was not enough. For seventeen years she tried to get me to go to counseling, to grow up! But I refused to listen to her; I even said, "This is who you married! Get used to it!" On December 25, 1994, Christmas Day, she told me that we were "definitely getting a divorce." The shock was earth shattering! It was the blow that finally got through to me, and for the first time, I looked at myself *honestly*. In March of 1998, having been divorced for about two-and-a-half years, I walked into an Al-Anon meeting to try to get help understanding alcoholism in a loved one. I was told I couldn't change anyone but myself, and as it turned out, your nanna had been right all along. I did need help. Since that day in 1998, I have been on a quest of inner discovery, of Truth seeking. If I know anything, it was learned—almost all of it—from that day forward.

Adulthood is not determined by age—I was forty-three years old in 1998 when I finally began the process of changing into an adult. Learn from my experience and start now! You will have a much better life, and sooner!

Important Note

In this letter, and in all these letters, and in all of life, *the choice is yours.* Again this is both a great freedom and a great responsibility. Consider *everything* thoughtfully.

I would be interested in hearing what you are thinking about. Give me a call with your thoughts.

With love,
Grandpa

Letter 7: Self-Respect

Don't leave home without it!

Dear Eddy and Alan,

The next two letters are going to cover things that I have struggled with all my life: self-respect and relationships, and they are closely related. I am still struggling with these issues. So, yes, I am not perfect. No one is (that I know), but I try not to let that be an excuse for not trying to be the best person I possibly can be.

What Exactly Is Self-Respect?
Self-respect is liking the person you are, feeling worthy of success and worthy of being loved. In letter 5, I wrote: "Believe in yourself: only if you feel worthy will you allow yourself to try to succeed." In letter 1, I wrote: "Be a person that you can be proud of!" When you look in the mirror, look in the eyes of that person and ask yourself, "Is this a

person that I like? What kind of character traits does this person have that make me glad to *be* this person? What kind of character traits does this person have that make me ashamed of being this person?" We all have work to do; each of us must become a good person in order to *like* the person we are.

Truth

The good news is that you have the freedom to decide who you want to be and the power to change who you are. The method I use, which has been successfully used by millions of people for about a hundred years, will be covered in a future letter: "Who Do You Want to Be?""

Why self-respect is important:

- In the letter just before this one, I wrote: "If you don't have self-respect, you have nothing." If you don't like yourself, you can never be at peace, because no matter where you go...you will be there.

- Not liking yourself can, and very often does, result in addiction to alcohol, gambling, drugs, and many other self-destructive habits. These things *destroy* people's lives, and it happens to a lot of people because a lot of people don't like themselves and want to escape life. How sad to *want* to sleepwalk through life. What's worse, you will never get any wiser, just older, if you are not paying attention to the lessons that life is trying to teach you.

- Self-respect is required before you can have healthy relationships. If you don't like yourself, you will enter relationships as less than a whole person or shy away from relationships altogether. Unless you get right with "the man in the mirror," your ability to be loving will be almost nonexistent because you will feel unworthy of being loved.

- If you don't like yourself, you will enter a new situation with timidity and fear or avoid new situations and be a hermit. (Been there, done that!)
- On the other hand, if you are proud of yourself, you have confidence. You have values of a high standard; you are at peace with yourself and the world at large. With all of that going for you, new situations will be approached with anticipation, confidence, and calm. You can step into leadership roles with those character traits.

So, why do I struggle with my self-respect? It is something I learned from my parents, especially my dad.

True Story about My Dad

My dad was the second youngest of ten children. His mother had a favorite child—her youngest child, Kenneth. While he was growing up, my dad was constantly reminded that he was not important to his mother. He claimed that he was raised by his oldest sister because his mother had abandoned him and gave all her attention to Kenneth. During World War II, both Kenneth and my dad served overseas: my dad in the army as a foot soldier in the Pacific theater, Kenneth as a navigator aboard a bomber in the skies over Europe. Kenneth's plane was shot down, and he was killed. (So I never met my uncle Kenneth.) My dad survived, one of the only 13 percent of his company that did. When he returned home after the war was over, his mother told him that the wrong son had been killed. Can you imagine that? My dad spent *the rest of his life* trying to prove her wrong—even after she died! The good news about this is that Dad had a spiritual experience just a few weeks before he died. He had a vision of his friend John, who had died a few years earlier, in heaven. John gave Dad a tour, and this experience gave my father peace. After eighty-seven years of not feeling good about himself, I believe that he accepted that he was OK, and that allowed him to finally find self-respect and die in peace. Learn from your great-grandfather: *seek to obtain self-respect now. Don't wait!*

The lack of self-respect is handed down from generation to generation.

The bad news about this tale is that, since his mother did not like my dad, she criticized him. So when I was growing up in my parent's house, I too got constant criticism because that is how both of my parents were trained to be parents by their parents. Further, both of my parents were emotionally distant from us kids: never a hug, never a "good job" or a "well done," never an "I love you." But always an endless stream of criticism, yelling, and hitting. Somehow, in all of this, I felt like they loved me even though it was never shown. This is why I struggle with self-respect. Only recently have I learned to be confident and believe that I am worthy of doing something well—I have even learned to enjoy speaking in front of an audience. I have, rather late in my life, broken the cycle of inherited self-loathing.

Take note: *I wish I had learned this at your age!* I would have been a much better husband to my wife and a much better father to my children. So it is important for you guys to make sure you have self-respect *now!* You can have better relationships, be a better husband, and be a better father. (Marriage and parenting are subjects of future letters—oh boy!)

How Does One Earn Self-Respect?

1. In my last letter, I said that self-respect begins with honesty—fanatical honesty! You must be totally committed to always being honest, with others and with yourself.

2. Providing for yourself and your family is foundational. That is also the subject of a future letter: "Work: Expect to earn everything you get in this life."

3. Always do your best—don't be lazy and perform below your ability. Performing below your ability is called doing yourself a disservice. That's because you cannot think well of yourself if you only do just enough to get by. This is important in school, work, family, and all relationships. Remember the lessons of letter 2.

4. Treat others as you would like to be treated. Your kindness will often be returned, and you will certainly have more friends and more fun! But you will also have the good feeling of being one of the good guys!

5. Think of others as your equals. Do not be arrogant or act superior. People who act like they are better than others are usually overcompensating for poor self-respect. People who are comfortable with who they are don't need to try to be superior or show off.

6. Do not think of yourself as less than others—never think of yourself as unworthy. You deserve to prosper, and you deserve what you earn. And, most importantly, you deserve to be loved—and you are!

Be a person that you can be proud of! Self-respect is critical to good relationships, to have peace, and to feel worthy of success. It is always important at every time in life. It is a big deal. Think about it.

With love,
Grandpa

Letter 8: Relationships

We were born to be in relationships with others, but it takes effort.

Dear Alan and Eddy,

This is the second letter that is about an area that I am weak in, and this one is the one I continue to struggle with the most: *relationships.* And yet I know that relationships are the most valuable thing a person can have. My problem, I think, is that I approach everything on an intellectual level. Things must be logical—they must make sense—for me to understand them. And having relationships is more of an emotional thing. My predisposition for logic may be a personality trait I was born with; it may be my upbringing or a product of both, but regardless, relationships are a weak area I need to improve in, and I am working on it.

Funny True Story

Your mother once told me (maybe in the year 2001—she was eighteen) that I was "socially retarded." And she was right! Her mother told me something similar about fifteen years before that when she was exasperated with me for not wanting to meet people and socialize with them. (See the True Story below.) It is still true today. I *know* on an intellectual level that I should be better at relationships, but I still don't do them well. I have been working on it with some success but still have a long way to go!

The subject of the letter before this one, "Self-Respect" (letter 7), is important to relationships. *You must like who you are before you can have good relationships.* So the two things, self-respect and relationships, are closely connected. I finished this letter soon after the self-respect letter because it was mostly written as I was writing the other.

True Story

In 1985, I was married to your nanna, and we had kids: your mom and your uncle. Your uncle was five years old, and he played on a T-ball team. We met the parents of one of your uncle's teammates, who became good friends of ours, your nanna's and mine. Maybe around 1986 these friends invited your nanna and me to an event at a fancy social club. The club was an association of the "elite" in town; all the rich, successful socialites were members. We spent the evening talking to these people (none of whom I knew), and I would rather have been in the dentist's chair having my teeth drilled! It was torture! When we got home, your nanna told me I needed to learn how to meet people... *and enjoy it!* It was not a good conversation, but in my heart, I knew she was right. My problem was not so much that I detested "putting on airs" and acting like I'm something special (which I still detest), but my big problem was that I had low self-respect and truly felt inferior to all those people. And to that extent, your nanna was right: I needed to do a lot of work on myself. I have done a lot of work on my self-respect, and I might do better in that situation now, but I would still have nothing in common with those folks so would never desire to be a member of the club.

This story shows how self-respect is critical to having relationships: my lack of self-respect was a *huge* stumbling block in my relationship with my wife, and it was a huge stumbling block in my relationships with others.

The importance of relationships cannot be overstated. In my life most of my joy has been found in relationships. Time spent with friends and family is the best time in my life. I hope you agree and that you can see the importance of relationships. The subtitle of this letter stated: "We were born to be in relationships with others, but it takes effort." I said that because it seems like something is missing when I am not seeing friends for a while, and I long to reconnect. Recently lockdown orders because of COVID-19 have resulted in a large increase in anxiety and depression.[6] People need connections with other people.

My Experience with Relationships

I was the youngest of six children and the only boy. My five older sisters were either too old for me to be close to or young enough that they enjoyed being mean to me and being smarter and bigger, etc. We seemed to have nothing in common either: they liked to play with dolls and toy horses; I liked to play with balls and toy cars. Because of this distance, I moved into the basement when I was in sixth grade (or thereabouts) and began my life as a hermit. I had friends; there were a lot of boys my age that lived in my neighborhood, and we played a lot of sports; we all shared an interest in building model cars. But when I built models,

I did it alone—and those times of solitude were times of peace and quiet, and I enjoyed that too. I was never uncomfortable being alone. To this day I enjoy being alone with my thoughts, writing them out... like I am doing right now. I can do this all day and often do.

My mom and dad were not a good example of how to do relationships either. They always had friends, but they seemed to change friends often over the years and never had best friends for life. So they didn't model for me how to do friendships well. I have been trying to learn how to do marriage better, and we will talk about that special relationship in a future letter.

A Huge Event in My Life

I learned on August 15, 1987, how important relationships are. I was putting posts under a steel beam for a house I was building. The post that I was adjusting began to lean. My first thought was that I had been screwing the wrong way (because the adjustment screw is upside down, and it's easy to get mixed up) and that the top of the post had come loose and was falling away from the beam, so I tried to catch the post before it fell all the way. When I couldn't stop it or even slow it, I realized the beam was coming down with the post. Three thoughts came into my mind: "Oh, shit! I'm dead. I'm glad I have good life insurance." I remember thinking those three thoughts very clearly as if it was yesterday.

My *reality* at that moment was "I am dead." In my mind I saw a table about the size of a card table. On it was an incredibly detailed model of a large city of skyscrapers. I could see every brick of every building and every baluster of every handrail on every balcony. I thought, "Somebody spent an incredible amount of time building this model." It came to me that the modeler was *me!* This ridiculously intricate model was a representation of my life's work along with the stuff that I thought was important. I don't know how I knew, but I knew as I still know today. Here was my business—all the houses I had built, my house and all its furnishings, my cars, vacations, status symbols of every kind, carefully crafted with many years of hard work and determination to create this magnificent *monument to me.* This was the ultimate *false idol: my stuff.* Suddenly it all turned to dust and was blown off the table as if a giant arm had swept it away—dust in the wind! Every physical thing I owned or had created in this world was gone! And since in my mind, I was dead, this is what really had just happened. But remaining on the table were my family and friends—loved ones. I hadn't seen them before because they were very small compared to all the other stuff that I had given so much importance to in my life. It was perfectly clear to me that *love is the only thing we will take with us when we leave this earth; everything else is just temporary. Love is the only lasting thing; it is the only thing that is important. It deserves our close attention and our diligent efforts to cultivate it—and to generously give it away!*

This all came to me in the blink of an eye, with incredible instantaneous insight. Perhaps it was my life flashing before my eyes. I believe the message is Truth. The message is simple, and it is logical—you truly can't take anything physical with you. What I know of Truth is that it is simple, and it is intuitive. When we see it, although it appears to be a great revelation, it's as if we already knew it but had forgotten it. Also it is contradictory to what the materialistic and self-centered world tells us. *Truth is hard to see because it is covered up so completely by materialism and egotism.*

But the steel beam wasn't big enough. It took an even greater amount of pain—the loss of my family through divorce—before I understood this: *it's not enough to know a truth; you have to act on it.* It still doesn't come naturally for me to express love, but I'm working on it.

Truth

Love is infinite. The more you give, the more you have.

True Story

Here is an example of how to be a good friend. A few months ago, I was working with my friend Kevin. I was talking to him about how my drill bit box was missing several drill bit sizes, and the drill bits I had were dull and old, and how I really needed to buy a whole new drill bit set. Well a few days later, Kevin handed me a new box of drill bits and said, "Here you go, Mike. Now you have a new box of drill bits." He was thoughtful and thought of me and did something for me that I was too cheap to do for myself. That is how to treat your friends. Now *I* need to go and do likewise!

Relationships are what life is all about: treating others as you wish others would treat you makes for good relationships, which makes for a great life. And as it turns out, it is the only lasting thing in life. Let the people you love know it. Tell them you love them, then go out of your way to treat them well. You will have a storehouse full of the greatest treasures on earth.

With love,
Grandpa

Letter 9: Beware!

Not all in this world is nice, fair, or equal.

Dear Eddy and Alan,

The subject of this letter is negative, but negative issues are part of life. *You must face negative issues so that you can deal with them.* Dealing with the ugly aspects of life, no matter what they are, allows you to learn and mature, which will result in a positive outcome. Never ignore an ugly issue in your life. Ignoring your issues will result in unintended consequences that can ruin your life. Like an untreated cancer, unresolved issues continue to grow and fester until they take over your life completely. Unresolved issues cause stress, and stress causes anxiety and even physical problems like high blood pressure, which can cause heart attacks and strokes. Unresolved issues often are the cause of dependencies: alcoholism, drug addiction, gambling, eating disorders, etc. If you want to avoid those things, always deal with your issues. Get professional help, if need be, and get them resolved!

True Story

I was in a deep depression from 1993 to 2000. I call it "my seven years in hell." It began with my house-building business going broke; it grew immensely when my wife divorced me because I was depressed and angry (unresolved issues causing bigger issues), and continued to grow through the years because I didn't get treatment. My depression was a time in which I was focused on myself and my emotional pain. It was a self-feeding sickness—the more I focused on my pain, the more intense the pain became, and that caused me to focus on the pain more. It got to the point where the only thing I thought about was my pain. The pain was far more intense than the physical pain I felt when the steel beam crushed all my ribs and a hip, broke my pelvis in eight places, and mangled my leg. My only escape from the pain was going to work. So that was my life: work and pain. (Fortunately I was a long haul truck driver and spent almost all my working hours alone and didn't bother other people very much.) I finally went to a therapist in 2000, and it took about eight weeks of more pain to work through a system of letting go. I went to another therapist about ten years later for more work on letting go, because I still held on to my hurt. It was a lot of pain that I didn't need to suffer if I had sought help sooner. *Do not be too proud to ask for help.*

On with the subject of this letter:

Not everyone is nice. In letter 6, I wrote: "If you get the feeling that something smells fishy, pay attention to that feeling!" There are people in the world who will try to separate you from your money. They are not good people, and you should be aware that they are out there in the world and watch out for them.

You Can't Cheat an Honest Man. In 1939 W. C. Fields (a comedian of the time) made a movie with that title—I don't believe I have ever seen it. I am familiar with the expression because my father used it a lot when I was young. I never figured out what it meant until I was in business for myself and met many people who were dishonest. Let me save you years of wondering what this statement means. It means that honest people expect to *earn* everything they get, so they are not likely to fall for a scheme that promises them a shortcut to wealth. But dishonest people, *people trying to take a shortcut to wealth, are susceptible to being scammed themselves.* (Watch the movie *The Sting* with Paul Newman and Robert Redford—great movie!) As an aid to your desire to *not* be cheated, be honest; *expect to earn everything you get in this life.*

There are a lot of things and people in this world that are painful and challenging. If you guys take everything that I am writing to you and apply it to your life, your life will be far better than average. *But* (this is important) your life will certainly *not* be perfect or pain-free. The reason I am writing these letters is to give you the benefit of my experience so that if you learn from my mistakes, you can avoid making the same mistakes I made and avoid some of the pain of learning these things the hard way. But there will still be pain in your life.

Example

In letter 2, I wrote: "As the driver of a car, you are responsible for the safety of yourself, of other people in the car, and of every other person in the vicinity. Don't ever forget that!" If you accept this as true and incorporate this idea into your approach to driving, you will be a safer driver and have fewer collisions. This will save a lot of trouble for yourself and other people, save you the pain of injury and worse, the pain of being responsible for someone else's injury or death, and ultimately could save your own life! That's the good news. The bad news is that it will not guarantee that you will never be involved in a collision while driving.

Truth

Pain is not completely avoidable; it is part of life. These letters cannot cover every situation you may come across, so you will discover truths of your own…through pain. The problems we experience in life, though painful, give us opportunities to grow in maturity and wisdom. *Our problems make us better* if *we are wise enough to learn from them.* From great pain comes great wisdom.

Truth

Life is not easy! Beware of your instinctive desire to want an easy life. The pursuit of "easy" ruins the lives of those who are lazy and greedy. Decide to earn your way through life, deal with its challenges, and work on your issues. *It is worth the effort!*

True Story

More on the steel-beam incident from letter 8. On the day the beam fell on me, August 15, 1987, I was thirty-two years old with two small children: your uncle, seven, and your mom, four. When the beam fell on me, the injuries were life threatening. While lying in my hospital bed, I figured out how the beam came to fall and was contemplating a lawsuit against the company whose employees had removed the crucial brace (that I had failed to check). My cousin had won a lawsuit stemming from a motorcycle collision a few years before, and he got a big settlement. He said that I could easily win an amount large enough that I would be financially set for life—*I would never have to work another day in my life!* At thirty-two with a wife and two children to support and an uncertain ability to work because I didn't know how well I would recover, it was an extremely attractive idea. My wife (your nanna) and I discussed it but did not make a decision right away. Alone in my hospital room, I was thinking that I would like to file the lawsuit, and I was thinking about how it would feel to have no money worries for the rest of my life. I was tempted to "push the easy button." Suddenly an image came to my mind of me shaving while looking in a mirror. I was shaving the face of a person who took a shortcut, a person who took the easy way out, a person who *cheated on life!* I realized that I didn't like that person. A thought came to my mind: "You should expect to earn everything you get in this life." The thought was not my own, but the Truth of it was perfectly clear. When my wife came to visit me later that day, I told her that we were not going to sue. She didn't say anything, which is very surprising, considering that I just made a mountain-sized decision that would affect both of us for the rest of our lives, and I made it without her! She never brought it up, even during our divorce in 1995 when I asked her to tell me why she was divorcing me. (The list was *very* long! And I had no defense for any of it!) She and I have never had a conversation on this subject since that day in the hospital, and that wasn't even a conversation—I just made a statement, and that was that. I don't know why she never brought it up…but maybe the Truth of it was clear to her too.

That decision to earn everything I get in this life was made in 1987. It has been thirty-five years since I made that decision. Have I ever regretted it? Yes. A few years later in 1990, my father approached me with an idea to develop some land he had and build some houses. The idea needed some cash that my father did not have. He tried borrowing it from my sister, but she refused. He asked me, and I was greedy enough to buy in. (I was looking for a shortcut. I wanted to get rich quick, *even though I knew better!*) I didn't have the cash, but I did own an ocean-front lot in Grand Cayman, which my father had given me in 1967. (An oceanfront lot like this is worth millions of dollars today.) I sold the lot and put the proceeds into the project, only to watch all that money slowly…go…down…the…drain. It took two years of struggle and pain to lose it all. A large portion of our net worth…gone! It was horribly depressing, and there were times I wished I had that money from a lawsuit because we were broke, except for our house, with no income. I started driving a truck to support my family in March 1993, and that temporary job ended up being the career of twenty-plus years, which defines me more than my building/developing business.

Now? How do I feel about my decision to earn my way through life? I am *hugely* grateful that I made that decision. *Everything* we own, Margaret and I have earned in the past twenty-two years. We were both basically broke when we got married, but thanks to Dave Ramsey's Financial Peace University (more on that in a future letter) and *a lot* of hard work, we have saved a good-sized nest egg. None of it inherited, no lottery win or lawsuit, no shortcuts or cheating. All of it earned.

You want to have the same feeling of accomplishment and self-reliance when you are old and looking back on your life. *You do not want to take the easy way out in life. You can never have self-respect if you do! This is huge!* Those who pursue an easy life or easy solutions to big problems are lazy. Those who take the challenges of life head on and do the difficult and often lifelong hard work are the successful ones. Successful in every way. There is an old expression: "You get out of life what you put into it." It is true! People who pursue "easy" lose out on *everything* that life has to offer.

Truth

Life is not fair! This is something that my father said to me often, *and* it is an important idea to understand.

True Story

I was the only boy and the youngest child, growing up with five older sisters. My father was at work most of the time, so that left me in a house full of women, all of them older, wiser, and with more education than me. Often I heard myself saying "That's not fair!" because I almost never got my way. If my father was home and heard me say this, he would respond with "Life is not fair!" That always seemed counterintuitive at the time. Children are idealists; they want the world to be nice, fun (always), and fair. So when my father said this with no further explanation, it aggravated me because it seemed like he just wanted to shut me up (which also may have been true), but it seemed, well… unfair! But at my stage of life now, I can see the truth of this statement. More importantly I can see reasons that it is harmful to me if I *want* life to be fair. So unlike my father, I am going to explain my view, and hopefully you guys will understand why it is a wrong approach to life to expect it to be fair.

It is impossible for life to be "fair" for everyone. Everyone has different ideas of what "fair" looks like. Just this morning I spoke with a friend at church who wished that there were no choices to make in life. He said that he was afraid that he would make the wrong decision; he wanted God to be in control of everything and make all his decisions for him. I, on the other hand, love my freedom and want to be in control of my life. Yes, it is more difficult to be responsible and to sometimes make mistakes and suffer the consequences, but it is the only way I can learn and grow. So what my friend sees as fair is the opposite of what I see as fair. We can't both have our way, because either we are responsible for our lives or we are not. It can't be both (letter 2). True enough, he can believe what he wants to believe, and I can believe what I want to believe, and we can be nice to each other and get along just fine. *But only one of us can be right.* And there is Right and Wrong (letter 5). I did not create my collection of interconnected beliefs. (I'm not that smart.) I only discovered them after *a lot* of searching.

The world works the same way for everyone. Some are born with great talents, and some are born with little talent; some are born into money, and some are born into poverty; some are born with good health, and some suffer with poor health from birth. While all people have different experiences in life, we all must live under the same truths that do *not* play favorites. *No matter what our backgrounds, we all have the same responsibility: to make the most of the life we were born into.* To waste time and energy complaining that someone else got a better lot in life than we did is futile and makes us victims. *You are never a victim unless you see yourself as a victim.* If you see yourself as a victim, you will be under the control of circumstances that *you believe* are beyond your control. You will be helpless. If you see yourself as free and empowered... you are free and empowered! Your powers will always be different from others' powers, but you still have control of you. Those who see life as fate or predetermined do not even have that! Learn how the world works, and you can be masters of life.

Do not compare yourself to other people. This is a losing game—you will lose every time! Either, in your mind, you are better off than someone else, and that makes you an elitist (or you feel guilty for being better off)—I've known a lot of people with unearned guilt; it warps your thinking. Or, in your mind, you see yourself as worse off than someone else, and that makes you angry at the unfairness. In either case, you lose! Yearning for "fairness" will create the desire for constant comparison of what you *perceive* others have or don't have. Instead, compare yourself to who you were yesterday. Strive to improve yourself every day! Everyone, especially you, benefits from the new, improved you!

Watch out for elements in our society that will try to play on your desire for "fairness." Advertisers are the worst at this. They want you to feel like you are the only person without a new car or new clothes or *something!* All they want is to sell you something, and they sometimes don't care how they do it. Politicians also use "fairness" as a ploy to get your vote. No one can provide fairness, because it is an impossibility, and they know that, but sometimes they don't care how they get your vote, just that they get it! *Always think for yourself* (letter 4).

This has been a long letter, but I hope it makes some points that make sense to you, and that you see how it could help you avoid some pitfalls of incorrect thinking. Like most Truths, the vast majority of people do not see or follow these beliefs because they do not come naturally nor agree with our selfish instincts. So if you follow this path, you will not be following the crowd, and that is good too! The person following the crowd eats a lot of dust!

Because of our selfish nature, we want life to be always nice, fun, and fair without doing anything to earn that. But instead, if you expect to earn everything you get through honest hard work, you will be well prepared to receive a better life. So in the end, you do get what you want! But your attitude must always be to *lovingly* serve others, or a better life will never happen for you. You must provide for your own living expenses, but don't spend all your money on yourself. Save some for giving; and save some time for volunteering. Because *serving only oneself is a guarantee for a miserable life!* Counterintuitive, I know, but nonetheless true. Try serving others and see if it works! More on that in a future letter.

Life is a precious gift. Don't waste it complaining that it isn't fair or being less than that of which you are capable. The decision, as always, is yours.

Think

Take time to be alone with your phone off and no distractions for at least twenty minutes at a time every day for a week. Spend this time thinking about your future.

I would be interested in hearing what you are thinking about.

With love,
Grandpa

Remember

- *Don't ignore the ugly issues of life.* The unintended consequences can be devastating!
- *You Can't Cheat an Honest Man.* You should expect to earn everything you get in this life.
- *Life is not easy.* To desire an easy life is a sure way to be disappointed and unhappy.
- *Life is not fair!* Don't expect it to be. Play the hand you were dealt to the best of your ability…with no complaints!

Letter 10: Pain, Grief, and Suffering

What to do with it; why it is necessary.

Dear Alan and Eddy,

This letter is a continuation of the last letter: "Beware!: Not everything in this world is nice, fair, or equal." That letter taught that there were dishonest people in the world and to protect yourself from them by expecting to earn everything you get in this life. This letter is a look at the inevitable experiences of pain, grief, and suffering that come with living as a human being on this planet. Learn to deal with the world on its terms and conditions, with your eyes wide open, and you will be prepared for hardship. *Get the big picture!*

Fubar: Fouled Up Beyond All Repair (This is not the original wording, but close enough.)

There are decisions we make in life that can never be reversed—there is no going back and undoing them. So please think carefully about the potential consequences of your decisions before making them. Sometimes the consequences will be with you for the rest of your life. Sometimes they can be life ending!

True Story

When I was fifteen, I had a bunch of good friends in my church youth group; one of them was Chester. He was sixteen, and he had a driver's license, so he would sometimes drive the group wherever we were going in his mom's old rusted-out Pontiac. It had large holes in the back seat floorboards. Those were fun times! Chester made a decision one evening to go for a ride with a classmate, Charley, who had a brand-new 1970 Chevelle SS 396. This was a very powerful and fast car (highly collectible today) in the hands of a sixteen-year-old! Not a good idea for Charley's parents (who probably wanted their darling child to have everything they never got), and you can guess what resulted. Charley was demonstrating to Chester and two other boys in the car how fast his new car would go on Thirty-Nineth Street, a two-lane country road with ditches on each side and no shoulders. He lost control, went into the ditch, and crashed the car. Chester suffered a head injury and died two days later; no one else in the car had any serious injuries. Chester's decision to go for that ride that night cost him his life: fubar! Alan and Eddy, let Chester's poor decision that night in 1970 be a lesson you can learn from: *be careful who you get into a car with!*

Life-altering Decisions

There are a lot of decisions you will be faced with in life that can have life-altering consequences. Make sure you consider *now* what those decisions should be.

- *Should I take up smoking?* Cigarettes are marketed to young people because young people make impulsive decisions. The decision to take up smoking is a decision every smoker I have ever had this conversation with regrets. But they're hooked!
- *Drugs or alcohol?* The same, except...*worse!*
- *Premarital sex?* Birth control is *not* 100 percent effective. If you get somebody pregnant, that is life changing! If you're married, that change to your life is a good thing. If not...then you are forced into major life-altering changes for you and her! Then there are sexually transmitted diseases, some of which are not curable; some can be fatal. Premarital sex is a big-time fubar! It will be covered in a future letter: "Dating, Marriage, and Sex."
- *Think* about any other potentially life-altering decisions you might be faced with. Decide *now* what your decision will be. Then when the choice presents itself, you will have already made your decision in a calm and rational way, taking all the time that a *big* decision requires. *Do not wait* until the situation requires a decision *right then,* before deciding. *Do not make a rash decision about a potentially life-changing issue.* Avoid, if you can, the pain, grief, and suffering the fubar situation could make of your life.

Assignment

Think about any decisions that you may be faced with in your life. Make a list of them. Consider the possible consequences of the possible various choices and make those decisions now! When the situation presents itself, you are ready with the best choice.

Even if you do all you can to avoid making bad decisions, as I said in the letter before this one, your life will certainly *not* be perfect or pain-free. There are imperfect realities that are a part of life: disease, tornados, car wrecks, death of loved ones, just plain old mistakes, etc. Having proper insurance protects you from the financial disaster these can cause but not the pain, grief, and suffering. So how does one deal with that?

How Can Good Come from Bad? (Because it can, you know.)
First, know that pain, grief, and suffering are a part of life. Do not pretend that life is "all good." You will be setting yourself up for disappointment. Instead, do what you can to make your life stable and mistake-free but know that bad things happen, despite your best efforts.

Second, know that there are important lessons to learn from failures and pain. When pain happens:

- *Do not* pretend that it doesn't hurt. Sweeping problems under the rug or denying they exist only causes *bad* unintended consequences. Do not hesitate to ask for help!
- Look for your responsibility regarding the problem. Own up to your mistakes and make amends where possible to anyone you may have hurt.
- Wrap your mind around the issue as completely as you can. Carefully consider the full extent of the problem and all its possible outcomes. Face the worst possible scenario and accept it; then decide how to move forward from there. This is how to conquer fear. I got this idea from Dale Carnegie's *How to Stop Worrying and Start Living.*[7]

- Do all you can to remedy or at least minimize the problem. List all the possible avenues you could take to solve the problem; choose the best one.
- Learn all the lessons the problem is teaching and adjust your behavior accordingly so that you don't repeat the same mistakes.
- What you are unable to remedy, you must learn to live with. Carry on with dignity and *without complaint!* Be grateful for what you have and move forward from there.
- *"If it doesn't kill you, it will make you stronger!"*[8] If it does kill you, your worries are over.

Example

Let's look at the steel-beam incident I mentioned in the two previous letters. In letter 8, I explained how I learned this lesson from the steel-beam incident: "Love is the only lasting thing; it is the only thing that is important." In letter 9, I explained how I learned this lesson from the steel-beam incident: "You should expect to earn everything you get in this life." Both of these important and powerful lessons were a benefit of the horrendous pain of being crushed under the steel beam. And from this letter, I also learned this lesson from the steel-beam incident: "If it doesn't kill you, it will make you stronger!" My psychiatrist gave this advice to me while I was in the hospital. It didn't kill me, and I am stronger from the experience. You guys are lucky; you don't have to experience the pain I experienced in order to learn these lessons. You can learn from my painful experiences. But you will experience pain of your own in your lives, so be ready to learn its lessons.

Remember

It is in living through our pain and learning from our mistakes that we mature and grow wise. These trials are necessary for our growth, but you can also learn from the mistakes of others…so be smart and pay heed! As you grow in wisdom (knowledge applied to life), others will learn from your example. *Be a leader!*

With love,
Grandpa

Letter 11: Who Do You Want to Be?

Each of us has the power to change ourselves into a better version of ourselves.

Dear Eddy and Alan,

In letter 2, I wrote: "Who you are is your responsibility!" It is your responsibility to change yourself into a better person. *Be a person that you can be proud of—a person who is loving and considerate and compassionate.*

Truth

The root of all evil is selfishness. This is a truth I discovered about eighteen to twenty years ago, and I have been testing it ever since. Try it for yourselves: think of an evil, then consider the motive for that evil. It is always selfishness in one form or another. Knowing this Truth allows you to discern what the correct behavior may be. Ask yourself: "Are my motives selfish or loving?" Do the loving thing, and you will be doing the right thing! This does not mean that you must accept bad behavior from loved ones; that is a relationship issue, not a question of love. You can still love someone and not be in a relationship with them.

Perhaps you believe that you are who you are, and nothing can change that. This is a common belief. If a poll were taken, I am willing to bet that most people feel this way. I too felt that way up until I was forty-three. (In 1998 I walked into an Al-Anon meeting.) In letter 6, I wrote that I told your nanna, when she was my wife and wanted me to change, "This is who you married. Get used to it!" I truly believed that at the time, but looking back on it now, knowing what I know, it was utterly stupid and motivated by my lazy desire to remain selfish. I hope you guys can understand how wrong I was then. If you see the foolishness of not wanting to change and not wanting to become unselfish, you will see the desirability of wanting to be a better, more mature, and loving person.

Truth

The biggest job in life, and the most rewarding job in life, is this: *each of us must change ourselves from perfectly selfish babies into loving, mature adults.* Adulthood has nothing to do with age (except in the eyes of the law).

Adult: "fully developed and mature."[9]

Mature: "of or relating to a condition of full development" and "characteristic of or suitable to a mature individual."[10] I would also add: a person having the characteristic of considering other people as equally important to themselves. Add it all up and you get the idea.

People do not change without an intentional decision on their part, a strong commitment to do the work, and the perseverance to see the work through *for the rest of their life*. Margaret and I both were very different (read "ignorant") people when we were young. We have both, separately and then together, made very intentional decisions to start doing life better and have spent the past twenty-four-plus years improving ourselves. If we look back on who we were forty years ago, thirty years ago, we shake our heads in shame and thank God for the gift of free will so that we can change who we are. It is our personal responsibility to change into better and better people. In my opinion the change from our natural selves (selfish) to our better selves (loving) is what life is all about. So *how* to do it is very important.

Truth

If I do nothing to change who I am, nothing will change. I will remain forever selfish.

How does a person become a new person?

How did Margaret and I do it? It took years of very intentional and challenging work! We met in 1998 at an Al-Anon meeting. We both did marriage wrong the first time and were divorced at the time. She had married an alcoholic; my first wife (your nanna) had married a spoiled brat with no self-respect. We became better, slowly, by working Al-Anon's Twelve Steps.[11] The Twelve Steps are a formula for recreating yourself, and they work. Here is my shortened interpretation:

1. Conduct a fearless *moral inventory* as described in letter 6. Ask others who are trustworthy to help you recognize your weaknesses and your strengths.
2. Write the moral inventory down so that you can refer to it and update it.
3. Work on only one error at a time, if you can, so you can focus.

4. Ask for forgiveness from those you may have hurt. Make amends if possible.

5. Decide to never behave in that manner again and change your behavior—even if you don't feel like it! Force your behavior to change using self-control. This is not easy!

6. *Continually* check your progress, retaking a moral inventory with trusted help.

7. When you discover another error, repeat the process. Update your written inventory.

8. Over time you will see improvement, but there is always room for more improvement, so keep working on these steps! And help other people work these steps too.

This process is also called repentance; we all need it continuously. I expect to be doing this until the day I die. In Al-Anon we ask ourselves: "Are you working the Steps?" because we know it is each person's responsibility. Nobody can do the work for us because the only person anyone can change is themselves, so no one can make me (or you) change. *It is each person's responsibility!*

As a result of following these steps, over time (maybe even years or decades), you will change not only your treatment of others but also how you think of others and yourself. Eventually you will become a new person. But if you do not engage in the process, you will never change.

My goal is to become perfect, treating other people with the same high degree of respect I hold toward myself. Will I ever reach that goal? Maybe not, but my goal is still perfection, and here's why:

I never want to set limitations on myself. Don't limit your thinking! Dream big! In letter 1, I wrote: "You can do whatever you set your mind to if you are willing to do the work necessary to make it happen."

If I limit my thinking as to how far I can go in my personal development, I will have established an excuse for failing to reach perfection, and, therefore, it will be impossible. Have you heard the expression "Nobody's perfect"? While the statement may be true, *it is an excuse for bad behavior.* Don't use it!

Never compare yourself to someone else. Comparing yourself to others is a losing game. You will see things in others that you don't have, and that will create *envy*. Or you will see flaws in others, and that will create a sense of *superiority* or give you an excuse to be less than you can be. All are wrong! Compare yourself to who you were yesterday. Are you a better person today? If so, you are going in the right direction, and you are a success.

Truth

Success is a journey, not a destination. If you are going in the right direction, you are a success. But don't stop the process of improvement. It's like riding a bicycle: if you are moving forward, you're doing well; but if you stop, you fall. Keep up the good work!

Be a person that you can be proud of. I know I have written this several times before, but I am being intentionally repetitious in the hope that the idea will be ingrained in your minds and cause some thinking. It is an awesome thought that gives each person the power to truly be who they want to be.

Remember

Is it loving, or is it selfish? The choice is yours. The future is wide open—carefully choose the paths you take.

With love,
Grandpa

This is an addition to the original letter:

Truth

Selfishness is self-destructive. The more we try to please ourselves, the more problems we will have. For example, *me!* When I was a young man and living life as I pleased, I made some vows to myself. One was a good vow, and it served me very well in a moment of tremendous temptation (which I will not detail here). That vow was "Because I am a man of honor, I will honor my marriage vows and never engage in an extramarital affair." (This has everything to do with self-respect.) When that moment of temptation arose, I had already made my decision, so I did not allow myself to give in. Because I had made the decision in advance, I didn't hesitate to do the right thing.

On the other hand, there were two vows I made as a young man that did not serve me well, and I believe it was because the *motive* for making those vows was selfishness:

1. "Because life is too short to not enjoy food, I am going to eat what I want." Because of this vow, I have battled with food addiction my entire adult life. I crave all the worst foods: pizza, barbeque, burgers, fries, ice cream, candy, etc. I am still trying to retrain my taste buds for wholesome foods. I am making slow progress.

2. "I am going to drive a nice car!" This resulted in numerous foolish purchases of "nice cars," which wasted *a lot* of money and caused me and my family to be broke *a lot* of the time and, in one case, meant I had no money for new clothes for the kids! This is a true story, as embarrassing as it is.

These two vows, serving my selfish nature, caused (and regarding food, still causes) me a lot of big problems. (I have controlled the new-car devil, but I am still tempted!) When making decisions, ask yourself,

"Is it loving, or is it selfish?" Also ask, "How will I feel about myself in the morning?"

Discipline, self-control, and sacrifice, while not pleasant at the time, result in getting what you truly want: financial stability, peace of mind, self-respect, and even, in the case of food, better health. Good reasons to *not* be selfish!

Letter 12: Utopia

Most people wish to live in a perfect society, but no one does. Why not?

Dear Alan and Eddy,

It is my belief that *most* people want many of the same things. We want to live in a society that is reasonably safe from criminals and that allows us to own property and earn for ourselves financial security, to love and be loved by others, and to have the freedom to set goals and accomplish them. Where things get interesting—to me at least—is when individuals try to get along with other individuals. As a group of individuals, we attempt to form a society where one's rights and freedoms do not interfere with the rights and freedoms of the others in the group. It is a very tricky business, as you can imagine. This letter is a look at those desires and how I believe they could be fulfilled.

A lot of people wish the world was perfect. I used to wonder to myself why the world wasn't perfect. Perhaps you do too. But now that I can look back on a lot of years of life, I can see a very good reason why the world is not perfect, and I am thankful—very thankful—that it is not. Because an imperfect world gives me challenges, and challenges give me work to do and avenues of growth through which I am strengthened and become wiser.

If I have no challenge to overcome, there is no potential for growth. I become spoiled and lazy. In the same way that my body needs exercise to stay fit and strong, I need challenges and failures to mature and learn. I know this sounds dreary and the exact opposite of fun, but you do want to grow wiser and stronger, don't you? In order to get what we want, we must discipline ourselves to do the work. (Next letter.)

Utopia: "a place of ideal perfection especially in laws, government, and social conditions."[4] Utopia is imaginary because it does not exist and has never existed in the known history of humanity. Utopia will never exist as long as humans are not perfect. People screw up. I do; you do; everyone does. If, in the future, human beings evolve and mature to the point that every single human is perfect, the world will be perfect except for natural disasters, and we will all be living in Utopia. Until that day happens, don't hold your breath. Instead *set your mind to dealing with the world as it is.* To hope for Utopia is a worthy goal, and to work toward personal perfection is an important task (letter 11), but don't spend a lot of time dreaming of Utopia and waiting for it to happen. Spend your time *doing* what you can to help it happen!

How Can Utopia Become Reality?

For a perfect society to exist, *all* people in that society must be perfect. We looked at the process of becoming a perfect person in the previous letter. Changing myself into a perfect person is a monumental task.

Everyone I have talked to about this, including several ministers whose job it is to help people become better people, have *all* claimed that it is impossible to be perfect. If it is of such great difficulty that making myself perfect is called *impossible* by experts, how hard do you expect it is to change someone else? Since I have no control over other people, then to make someone else perfect, I am willing to concede, is impossible. So society cannot make people become perfect. Therefore, to create a perfect society, I must first attempt to make myself perfect and help others who are willing to try to change themselves to do the same. Talk about a big job! *But it cannot be forced!* It must be voluntary on the part of each individual.

The Perfect Person

What would the perfect person be like?

- A person that cares about other people as much as themselves.
- A person who is completely willing to dedicate everything they have to help other people.
- A person that always said and did the loving thing.

Although I am not perfect yet, believe it or not, I have come a long way from the person I used to be, and I thank God that I am not that person anymore! Daily I make it one of my goals to improve myself. Imagine what the world would be like if everyone was committed to self-improvement! It might not be Utopia, but it would be going in that direction.

So don't move, trying to find Utopia! My friend dreamed of living in Florida since I met him in 1980. We had a falling-out about eleven years ago because of his dishonesty, but I happened to see him at the hardware store about a year ago. He and his wife had both retired and were getting ready to move to Florida after dreaming of it almost their whole lives—at least for the last forty years! But I doubt if he is any happier there than he was here if he is still the dishonest person he proved himself to be. I personally know people who fight like crazy to change society but do nothing to change the horribly selfish person they *can* change—themselves. Don't be that person.

Truth

Utopia begins with you. If you don't like yourself, you can never be happy, no matter how close to perfect society is, wherever it is that you are living. *Be a person that you can be proud of!* Change what you can change: you. This is a recurring theme, starting with letter 1. I restate this sentence because it is an incredibly important idea. How you think of yourself is *key* to how you treat other people and whether you enjoy life! *If you don't like who you are, you will not be happy.* This seems obvious when written out, but there are a lot of unhappy people in the world who never considered the fact that they hold the key to happiness in their hands. The *good news* is that you can change, but you are the only person that can change you. How can you accomplish being proud of yourself? Guard your self-respect with rigor! Always be honest. Admit it when you make a mistake and change your behavior, so you won't make the same mistake again.

True Story

My personal experience of seeking to live in Utopia: In May of 1980, your nanna (my wife of three years at the time) and I moved into an experimental community that was attempting to be ideal. At the time we moved there, the community had approximately thirty families living there. Basically the idea was for each home to be modest in size on a very small lot and for the community to own all the open space.

We cooperated on the maintenance of the grounds and the building exteriors. The main idea was for each family to be generous and give to the betterment of the community. And it had worked for about nine years before we got there because everyone in the community had that generous attitude. Then about a year after we got there, one family moved in that had the attitude of taking advantage of that generosity. They acted like they owned everything and were dishonest in their dealings with others (including me). The community declined after that. All it takes is one bad attitude to ruin something that was very nice—not perfect but nice. Generosity will fade when someone's desire to be a freeloader becomes apparent. *Every person* must be a giver for cooperation to succeed.

Your satisfaction in life is not dependent on external things. The society in which you live cannot make you happy. Fix what is wrong with you; do your best for society by being generous and living in service to others (more on that in a future letter), and you will be well on your way to having a great life filled with great friends! And the world will be a little bit closer to being Utopia. Spread the word by telling others and by your example. Who knows what could happen? Seek Utopia by living it out in your own life, and things will be better for you and for those around you. It's a win, win, win!

With love,
Grandpa

Letter 13: Work

Expect to earn everything you get in this life.

There is a lot of self-respect to be gained from providing for your own welfare. Work at something you love doing, and it will always be a joy to go to work!

Dear Eddy and Alan,

Messages from my mother (your great-grandmother):

1. "Hard work is its own reward." There is nothing like the feeling you get when you can look back on your day and see what you have done—it is a great feeling of accomplishment and a huge boost to your self-respect.

2. "Any job worth doing is worth doing well!" This has everything to do with self-respect—you do your best because you cannot have self-respect if you do shoddy work.

3. "Good morning! The sun is shining, the birds are singing, and there's work to be done!" This is how my mother woke us up on Saturday mornings—ugh!

4. "Life is work!" If you expect life to be easy, you will certainly be disappointed. The sooner you accept this fact, the better your life will be.

My mother grew up on a farm in southern Alabama, just north of the Florida panhandle, during the Depression. They worked to eat! No work...no food! Life was *no nonsense!* When I was a child, she was a taskmaster, that's for sure, but she taught me to work! And I thank God I learned that good old-fashioned *work ethic!* It is in short supply these days, and the world is the poorer for it. *Somebody* has got to do the work, or it doesn't get done. If the work doesn't get done, we all starve! The food in the grocery stores comes from farmers producing, warehouses storing, and truckers delivering.

True Story

Even though I was taught the work ethic, I was also spoiled. This story is the second half of the story I started in letter 2. The day I turned sixteen years old, in 1971, was the most anticipated day of my life up to then. The first thing I wanted to do that day was to get my driver's license, and I got my driver's license that morning.

Later that same evening, I *expected* to receive for my birthday present...a new car! (I was very spoiled. It has taken me most of my life to repair that damage.) Months earlier I had picked up a new 1971 car brochure at the Oldsmobile dealership. The brochure was big and beautiful (I wish I still had it), and it covered the Cutlass (midsize) line of cars. There were two-door and four-door cars, wagons, and convertibles, but in the back was the 4-4-2, the fast Cutlass with a big engine—455 cubic inches of displacement! These were the exciting times of what became known as the muscle car era. (I still subscribe to a magazine called *Muscle Machines*.) I used that brochure to create my ideal car. I chose a convertible with the high-performance W-30 engine, close-ratio four-speed manual transmission, limited-slip differential, blue exterior and a white interior. Almost all the options were checked. (I said "no, thank you" to body side moldings and door edge guards, nothing else.) I gave this to my dad a couple of months before my birthday so that he could get it ordered, and I fully expected to receive it on my birthday.

On the morning of my birthday, my dad told me not to go into the garage when I came home from school that afternoon. And he parked his car in the driveway instead of its usual place in the garage, and he even locked the man door into the garage, so I had to come into the house through the front door, which we seldom used.

At supper that evening, it was a birthday tradition for us to eat first, then have cake and ice cream, and then open presents. I could hardly eat my supper or the cake and ice cream. My stomach was tied in knots with anticipation of my new car! *Who can eat at a time like this?!* My dad told me that we would go to the garage last after I opened all my other presents. I hurriedly opened them (I have no idea what I received), and finally it was time to go to the garage. My dad walked behind me. I opened the door, and I looked into the garage. And there…under the lights of the garage…was my very own…brand-new…*lawnmower!* Boy, was the joke on me!

The reason my dad didn't get the car for me was because I probably would have killed myself in it and because he believed I had not *worked for it and earned it*, and he was right on both counts. The lawnmower represented the work I needed to do to earn a car. It was actually a great gift! But I sure didn't appreciate it at the time.

Funny note: I never got my dream car. At that time it would have retailed for around $5,000. That car today, if it was in good condition, would be worth $150,000 or more.

Truth
What you deserve in life is what you have earned.

From letter 3: "Make plans for a potential career path. What work would you like to do for the next forty-five years (including education) if you're like most people (Plan A)? Or what work would you like to do for the next twenty-five years if you live well below your income and save money aggressively (Plan B)? I would recommend Plan B." More on how to plan for financial independence in letter 15.

What Work Is Mine to Do?

1. *The number one job* of every human being (whether they know it or not) is to work at becoming a better person. This is not a popular idea. In fact almost *no one* wants to look at themselves critically and change themselves. Sometimes people are unwilling to look at themselves until their life becomes intolerable (me included: see True Story in the "Dating, Marriage, and Sex" letter). However, you guys can be different. Look at yourself now while your lives are relatively carefree instead of waiting for a monstrous tragedy that forces you to do it at a time of great crisis and great pain. This job of self-improvement is lifelong because the goal is perfection. The challenge is great, and the work of changing oneself is difficult, but the reward is living a life that is a life to the full.

2. *Earning your way through life.* Working for an employer or in your own business is how you earn money to pay for your living expenses: food, rent, utilities, transportation, etc.

3. *Career choice.* Consider what you enjoy working at. If there is a good living to be made doing it, that would be a good career choice. *Realize that the work you do in your career is of service to your fellow man, and it will always be a joy.* I discovered this while driving a truck. Do not do work that diminishes people. For example, a card dealer at a casino.

4. *After my career, what do I want to do?* It seems too soon to think about retirement when you are seventeen years old…or is it? As you consider your vocation, also consider your life after retirement, and you will make that a part of your life plan. Consider this: your career is supporting yourself and your family and preparing for retirement. Your retirement can be a time of your most important work if your work is loving service to your fellow man. *This is very fulfilling!* It is the subject of the "Halftime" letter.

Do not take shortcuts! Earn your money honestly, or you will have no self-respect. I have known people who were dishonest, and I feel sorry for them because either they are lazy or they do not think they are talented enough or smart enough to earn their way through life.

Truth

Expect to earn everything you get in this life. This is at least the fourth time this has been presented, but it bears repeating. Remember the lessons your great-grandmother taught me, at the beginning of this letter.

Work does some big jobs in your life:

1. It is the main method of paying for your living expenses…and creating wealth.

2. It gives you a sense of purpose—a reason to get out of bed in the morning.

3. It creates a sense of accomplishment, which contributes a great deal to your self-respect.

4. As a member of the human race, I believe that it is your obligation to do what you can to grow the wealth of the world—to be a producer. Otherwise, you are living on the results of someone else's work. It kind of defeats any purpose in your existence.

Work at something you love doing, and it will always be a joy to go to work!

With love,
Grandpa

Letter 14: Recreation

―――――――――――

After the work is done, it's time to relax!

Dear reader,

By the date on this letter, you can tell that it is not one of the original letters. Yesterday, the day after submitting my "complete" manuscript to the editors, I was riding my bicycle. This is my (not quite) daily exercise that you will read about in letter 17, "Health." But I was thinking about this book and the very first letter where I wrote the following:

"Achievement is not easy, but it is highly satisfying.
1. Set goals.
2. Create plans to accomplish those goals.
3. Go to work, and work, work, work to make it happen.
4. Don't forget to have fun too! But do your work first."

This made me think. I wrote a lot about work, but not much about having fun! And fun is important too. So it seems appropriate to put a new letter in the book that addresses "What about fun?" So I called the publisher and said, *"Stop the presses!"* There's some fun right there!

True Story

One thing that my dad placed a high priority on was having fun! Both of my parents were hard workers: my mom at home raising six children and keeping a large house clean (with the help of us kids, of course), and my dad running a business that for some years averaged building more than one house per day. That kept him busy! Before I started kindergarten, and after that in the summer, I would go with him to work quite often, and I loved doing that. To this day the smell of freshly dug dirt and freshly cut lumber takes me back to those times. However, my dad liked to take long vacations too. He would drive his business partner nuts, leaving in the middle of summer for six weeks in a row. But from my dad's point of view, summer vacations were not to be missed! Dad also liked taking the managers of the company on fishing and hunting trips and having company parties to eat the spoils. Anyone who wore a necktie got it cut off! The people who worked for my dad, plus their families, were like a large extended family. Those were some fun times! It taught me to take some time off and unwind.

I may have learned too well. When my kids were little, we went on vacations a lot, even if we had to pay for them with a credit card. (Not good.) My second wife, Margaret, and I started out doing that too: our honeymoon was paid for with credit cards, and we took a cruise one time when we were both between jobs...on a credit card. Those days are over, thank goodness! (See letter 15.) We pay cash now, but we make sure to take a vacation or two every year.

Weekends are a time to relax too. Even daily, one should take a walk or a bike ride and/or relax in the evening before going to bed. "All work and no play makes Jack a dull boy!" I was told this when I was young, and I never argued with it. But remember, get your work done first!

Personal Safety

Believe it or not, while on the same bike ride yesterday that I was talking about above, I thought of another subject I only touched on in my letters. While riding the bike trail (*never on the road*), I ring my little bell to warn pedestrians on the trail that I am approaching from behind. I am appreciative when those I warn raise their hand in a wave to acknowledge that they heard me and (maybe) to thank me for the warning. But most of the time this doesn't happen. Why? Because most of the pedestrians and bicyclists have earbuds in their ears and can't hear me. This is both rude and dangerous. Letter 9 warns that there are bad people in the world and to look out for them. A big part of that warning has to do with *personal safety.* It is called *having situational awareness.* Look around; pay attention to your surroundings. Know where you are, where you are going, and who is around you—all around you.

Do not put yourself in a dangerous situation. We hear a lot about missing cruise ship passengers. A lot of the time, it seems like they were seen last in the bar at two o'clock in the morning and were drunk. Someone once told me "Nothing good happens after midnight." Don't put yourself in that situation or any other situation that a reasonable person would deem dangerous. This requires you to be aware and to be thoughtful.

Who is responsible for your safety? You are! The police cannot be everywhere, keeping an eye out for your safety. If you walk into an unsafe situation because you are not thinking about your safety, and you find yourself in a dangerous place that you can't get out of, call 9-1-1, but it may be a while before help can arrive. You don't want to be in that situation; it is far better to avoid it in the first place. That requires situational awareness, and that requires you to pay attention to what you are doing.

When I was a truck driver, I was required to attend quarterly safety-training meetings. *While driving, safety is the number one priority!* But there was also training about safety while not driving, like walking through a dark parking lot at the truck stop, walking on ice in the winter, and even climbing in and out of the truck safely. It *all* has to do with *paying attention!* Look around you, take mental notes, look for possible danger, and most importantly, think—keep your mind on what you are doing and where you are going. Most people want to listen to their music and glue their noses to the video screen of their phones while walking, and it is not just rude to the people around them, it is dangerous.

There is a driver-training company that I learned about while I was a truck driver, called Smith System. They have five keys of safe driving. I still have them memorized, but I won't name them here because I would need to get their permission. But I found their system to be extremely helpful in building safe driving habits. As an on-the-road driver trainer and as a classroom trainer with the trucking companies I worked for, I taught hundreds of drivers those five good driving habits. The funny thing is, those same five safe driving habits apply equally well to any situation when you are around other people: walking on the bike trail, in a crowd, in a restaurant, etc. Go to their website and learn these,[12] or better yet take their safety class. It is very valuable for anyone.

As a student in a training class once—a class teaching me how to teach truck driving safety—I was given a statistic: 94 percent of all driving collisions involve driver error.[13] That means that if people were better trained and paid better attention, 94 percent of all driving collisions could be avoided. Think about that next time you drive.

Truth

Your personal safety and the safety of those around you are your responsibility! The good news is that you have a lot more control over your own safety than you may think. The bad news is that you cannot expect the other guy to keep you safe. Pay attention!

With love,
Grandpa

Letter 15: Money and Wealth

Work hard and you will have a good income—spend it wisely!

Dear Alan and Eddy,

This subject is one in which I have a great deal of personal experience, but it is one that one short letter cannot hope to cover adequately. So I will share with you some of my experience and recommend sources where you can get more information.

True Story

For most of my life, until I was fifty-one, I was spending every dollar I had and a lot of dollars I didn't have (I was borrowing). For most of my adult life, I was broke, in debt, and on the brink of financial disaster! The sad thing is (I didn't know it at the time) almost four out of five Americans are in this same mess.[1] Let me tell you, *it is a nightmare!*

However, in 2006 when I was fifty-one, I met Dave Ramsey (on the radio). He is a financial advisor whose website is *ramseysolutions. com.* Everything changed for me. Margaret and I started listening to his radio show. We read his book, *Total Money Makeover,*[14] and we took his class, Financial Peace University. Then we lead the class about a dozen times. We learned how to handle money, and helped a lot of other people do the same. I wish I had learned how to handle money when I was your age. Almost everyone middle aged and above who takes the class says the same thing. *Right now,* you have a *tremendous opportunity* to be financially secure for the rest of your life. This would be a great blessing for you. Please do yourself a huge favor—*learn this stuff!*

In brief, here is what we learned:
1. *Spend less than you make.* This requires making a budget every month and tracking every penny you spend to make sure you are staying on budget.
2. *Never use debt.* Don't give your money away to creditors—you get nothing for it. Never use debt except maybe to buy a house *under the right circumstances.*
3. *Save for emergencies, big purchases, and retirement.*

Then we went to *work!* You might recognize this word from letter 13. We cut our expenses to the bone, drove our *used* cars until the wheels fell off, and ate beans and rice. It was all about sacrificing our comforts and wants for our financial future. We went to work at our jobs like our lives depended on those jobs, because they did! Nothing about this is easy, but nothing worthwhile is easy!

It worked! Now sixteen years later, we have no debts, and we are nearly ready to retire with financial security. We went from broke to near financial independence in sixteen years. You can do the same thing! If you guys start now—getting your education and/or job training by *working at your studies like your life depends on it*, starting your careers, and *working at your jobs like your life depends on it*—if you follow Dave Ramsey's other financial advice in his book and class, you guys can retire young! *Or* keep working—your choice! But the sooner you start, the sooner you can have financial independence.

"If you will live like no one else, later you can live like no one else." -Dave Ramsey[15]

The time to start these habits is…*now!*

How will you pay for your education?

Your grandma and I have a small scholarship fund for both of you to share. It will help, but it may not be enough to get you the education that you want." *There are restrictions on how you will be allowed to spend this money:*

1. It must be for education, and the education must be in something that will translate into a job for which employers are going to be hiring. The last time we talked about careers, Alan wanted to be a plumber, which there is a strong demand for, so that qualifies. We would be happy to help pay for plumbing trade school. And Eddy wanted to get a degree in finance, which is also a career field in high demand, so that qualifies also. An example of a course of study that does not qualify would be Middle Eastern art history—I would need to be convinced that there is a demand for employees with that degree. If you don't know what you want to do careerwise, take a few years, work and support yourself, get some experience, and think about it. Your education needs to be a part of your overall life plan.

2. You guys will have to agree between yourselves how much your education will cost each of you and how you would like to divide the scholarship fund between you.

You each will need to figure out how you will pay for the rest of your education if this fund is not enough. I strongly suggest that you *do not borrow* for your education. If you borrow for your education, you will start life in a financial mess that will be a burden for many years. On Dave Ramsey's website is a book on how to finish school with zero debt titled, *Debt Free Degree* by Anthony ONeal.[2] If you want it, I will send it to you.

Truth from Letter 13
"What you deserve in life is what you have earned."

Money is for three things:
1. *To support yourself and your family.* You don't have to make a lot of money; the important thing is to spend much less than you earn so that you can save. Never let other people's opinions control what you do for a living (as long as it's honest and ethical) or how you spend, or don't spend, your money.
2. *To save for retirement.* Your retirement savings will provide income after the career is over, so you can pursue your passions in retirement regardless of whether it pays well.
3. *To give to charity.* Be generous! It is a key to being a person you can be proud of. Be careful who you give to, for some charities spend more on overhead than on charitable services. Do your homework before giving. But truly, "...giving is the most fun you can have with money!"—Dave Ramsey.[16]

How to Begin

I would recommend that you start with what Margaret and I started with, Dave Ramsey's book, *Total Money Makeover*,[14] If you would like a copy of it just let me know, and I will send you one. It is literally worth *far more* than its weight in gold! (I did the math.) Read the book, apply its principles to your finances, work, work, work, and see what happens.

Truth

The most important thing to know about money is your attitude toward it!

- If you are greedy, money will be a curse for you because you will never be satisfied with what you have. If having a lot of money is your goal, you will never have enough!
- If you are greedy, you will be operating on the assumption that money will make you happy. But since money can never make you happy, you will always be unhappy.
- If you are greedy, you will never know if people like you or *your money.*
- If you are greedy, the more money you have, the more miserable you will be because it will slowly become clear that you have spent your life pursuing a false belief, but since you have always believed it, you won't want to admit it...and change. You will instead say to yourself, "Money *will* make me happy! I just need *a little more* of it." (This was me!)

Truth

The correct attitude about money and wealth—assume it all belongs to God!

- Since it isn't yours, and you are only managing it for God, you will want to manage it well. You will want to be generous and compassionate with what you have.
- Since it isn't yours, there is no reason to try to impress people with what you have.
- Since it isn't yours, there is no reason to fight over it.
- Since it isn't yours, and what other people have isn't theirs, there is no need for:

  Jealously—the fear of losing what one has.

  Envy—the feeling of wanting what someone else has.

  Greed—the feeling of never having enough, even if one has plenty.

  Guilt—the feeling that it's not right to have money if others in the world are poor. This will cause a person to believe that they *should* be poor.

  Lack—the feeling that there is a limited supply of wealth and not enough of it in the world, so that if someone else has more, it means I have less. This will cause a person to delight in the misfortune of others. (Wealth is created from ingenuity and labor. There is no limit to the world's wealth. Go out there and create something that people want, better yet, need!)

Change your attitude about money and you will be rid of all that nonsense!

Money is a tool you use to get what you need to survive and hopefully thrive! *It is neither evil nor worthy of worship.* It is the necessary medium of exchange we need to live and conduct business. If your attitude toward money is correct, and you handle money well, you will hardly think about money at all. You will have financial peace!

Truth

If you handle it poorly, money will be the only thing you will be able to think about! I know this from personal experience. I was broke for many, many years; I didn't want to go to the mailbox because there were bills in there I couldn't pay. Broke is a horrible place to be! Learn the right way to handle money and the right attitude toward money, and you will be blessed with abundance. Do it now, and your whole life from now on will be blessed.

With love,
Grandpa

Letter 16: Be In-Service to Others

The biggest secret and the greatest joy in life!

Dear Eddy and Alan,

In letter 2, I wrote: "Do all you can do to alleviate the problems of the world. As a citizen of the world, it is your responsibility to help those who need help to the extent that you are able. Be careful; there is a right way to help and a wrong way. This is a long story and will be covered in a future letter but, briefly, don't just throw money at the problem. Money by itself solves nothing in the long term—it creates dependency. Give your time, over a period, establish relationships and trust, and require accountability. Then lasting change for the better can happen."

It seems to me that most people really want the same thing. We want a life that is peaceful, fulfilling, and content. Where we differ is in our approach to achieving that goal. A lot of people seem to believe that this goal will be achieved by changing society. This can only work if society controls your life—which it does not, thank God! On the other hand, I believe that this goal will be achieved by changing myself as discussed in letter 11, thereby changing society as discussed in letter 12. But there is another aspect of this we have not explored: our *attitude. Do I want to serve myself, or do I want to be in-service to others?*

It's 3:00 a.m. on Saturday morning, and I've been up for three hours. (My neighbor came home at midnight and decided it would be a good time to ride his motorcycle, which has no mufflers of course, up and down the street.) I am playing FreeCell and seeing parallels between the game and life. I don't know if you guys have ever played it, but it is a solitaire card game that is on every computer that I have ever used that has a Windows operating system. The object of the game, according to the rules, is to build stacks from ace to king in the top-right four cells in each of the four suits. If you play the game with this object in mind, you will lose most of the time. If instead, you attempt to build stacks on the eight columns the cards are dealt in, from king on the bottom to deuce on top, you will win a lot more often. (I haven't lost in the last 6,600-plus games.)

Truth

Change the objective, and you change the outcome. Life is like that!

What we perceive to be the objective of life is one thing, but it should be something else. Most of us believe that pleasing ourselves should be our goal in life, and that perspective will cause our attitude to be selfish, which will result in a miserable life and a poor life outcome. Becoming a better person should be our goal in life. From letters 2 and 11: "Who you are is your responsibility!" It is your *responsibility* to change yourself into a loving, compassionate human—a lifelong task! With that perspective, our attitude will be far better, and that will cause our behavior to be better, and the outcome of our life will be far different—far better!

There are important things all children should be taught but usually are not because their parents are too young to know any better. These things are the subjects of these letters, and the reason I know them is because I have lived a long time—doing things *wrong* most of that time. But I had to face the truth enough times that I finally learned some of it.

Truth

Serving oneself is the road to misery. Serving others is the most joyous thing in this life!

You cannot be happy serving yourself because someone else always has more stuff or a better life—or at least it appears that way—so you can never win that game. Helping people who need help is a win-win situation because, while it helps someone else, it gives you a good feeling too!

Be careful how you help. In letter 2, I said, "Be careful; there is a right way to help and a wrong way." You cannot simply throw money at a problem. First, you must have a relationship with the person you hope to help. They must trust you for them to believe what you are saying and follow your advice. This takes time—a month at least—just to gain the trust that is necessary. Second, there must be a method of accountability. Without accountability nothing is measurable, and it ends up just being a series of nice conversations. But ultimately you cannot change them (as we have discussed several times). They must change themselves, which means that *they must want to change.* This is a very brief look at a very big issue. The best books I have read on charity are *Toxic Charity* by Robert D. Lupton[17] and the sequel, *Charity Detox,* by the same author.[18] These books, if you truly want to help others, give you the secret (which I outlined above) of how to do it right. I recommend them most highly!

According to Dave Ramsey, 78 percent of Americans are living paycheck to paycheck.[1] They are spending everything they earn. Since they are spending all they make, they are probably spending it all on themselves. Personally I am very familiar with this mode of living; I wrote about it in letter 15. I did a lot of stupid stuff as a young adult, which I now regret. Margaret and I are lucky enough to have learned the joy of generosity and service. If you learn this secret of life, yours will be a blessed life!

Society and the media provide a lot of misinformation. We are constantly bombarded with advertisements about how we should indulge our selfish interests—it's on TV, radio, billboards, and the internet. It's even within the entertainment itself: the movies, books, and TV programs. Almost anywhere you look, you will find a selfish message. In the sixties the hippies used to say, "If it feels good, do it!" Those hippies are my age or older, and a lot of them have never learned any better. Even a large majority of churches teach the selfish message of instant and everlasting salvation, no matter what you do with your life. It is *all* a lie!

On the other hand, some movies and books have a strong message of courage in the face of danger and self-sacrifice for the benefit of others: *Lord of the Rings* and *Star Wars* (at least the original trilogy) are good examples. I believe that these kinds of books and movies are very popular because they speak to something in each of us that wants good to triumph and evil to be defeated. We admire courage and self-sacrifice, but it seems, after being exposed to these heroic messages, most people leave the theater and go about living their lives for their own selfish interests, never giving it a second thought. Wouldn't it be awesome if people would learn from the heroes of these fictional stories and put those values to work in their lives? What a different world it would be!

But as you know, we cannot control other people. Each person must decide for themselves. So I plead with you to learn from my advice. Take these lessons, apply them to your life, and see if they work. Be intentional about who you are and how you treat others. Be generous, considerate, kind, compassionate, and courageous. Be in-service to your fellow man. You will feel better about yourself, have better relationships, and have a significant positive effect on the world. If you do this, even society will be incrementally changed for the better! People will wonder why you are always smiling.

This subject, *what attitude do I want in my approach to life*, is challenging because it is not human nature. But if you get it wrong, your life will be miserable. As mine was before I figured it out. If you get it right, your life will be a joy—still hard work, but joyous work!

The Root of It Is a Simple Truth

The root of all evil is selfishness. This I mentioned in letter 11. The thought occurred to me one night about twenty years ago, while I was contemplating the meaning of life. The logic of it seemed instantly clear to me, but it took about ten years of testing it before I came to call it Truth. I have never found, in myself or in the world, something that is obviously evil—genocide, murder, slavery, rape, incest, stealing, lying, cheating, etc.—where the motivation for it could be anything other than selfishness. A tiny fib might have the motive of not wanting to hurt someone's feelings, but make sure that is your motive…better yet, say nothing! Don't take my word for it; test it yourself. I gave this

Truth to my pastor one time, challenged him to test it for himself, and a few months later I heard him use it in his sermon!

How is this Truth helpful? Firstly, it helps me gauge my own behavior and motives. Like everyone else, I was born with an ego, and that ego pops up every so often and causes me to do, say, or think something stupid and selfish...and I realize it if I am looking for it. So I try to keep looking for selfishness in myself and then correct myself.

Secondly, knowing the misguided motives of the evildoers of the world allows me to not hate them. Though we still require criminal penalties, I do not judge harshly because I too am often motivated by selfishness. If I can see that something a friend is doing is selfish, I can lovingly suggest alternative thoughts and maybe help them. This is tricky business, and I am not very good at it, let me state! But I'm working on it.

Right there is another example of selfishness being evil, because it is easier for me to ignore other people's selfish behavior than to try to help them become better people. Because of the potential hurt feelings and damage to our friendship, it is a big risk, so it is easier and less risky to ignore it and say nothing. That is selfish of me, and my friend does not get the opportunity to improve themselves. This is also an example of an evil that is an intentional omission of giving help. It's everywhere... but it is in my heart! Since it is me (my ego), I have absolute power to control it.

Margaret and I have a twenty-two-year history of being in-service, and it has been a huge source of joy in our lives. As soon as Margaret retires, we plan to be in-service for the second half of life. This will be the subject of a future letter. The thought of being in-service full time puts a smile on my face as I am writing this.

Of note, before you can give a lot of money to charity, make sure you are financially able. But right now even a small gift can help and bring you joy. Small gifts now will get you started on a lifetime of joyous giving and serving!

With love,
Grandpa

Letter 17: Health

Good diet, exercise, and sleep, plus avoiding drugs, alcohol, and smoking, maximizes your health so that you don't suffer a slow, painful death at a young age!

Dear Alan and Eddy,

Of all the subjects I am writing about, this is probably the most boring subject for you. (I hope these haven't been too boring.) Before I start on the subject of health, ask yourself a question: "What kind of life will I have if I am sick and feeble?" Obviously it will not be as good a life as it would be if you feel good and are energetic, wouldn't you agree? You might also be asking "How much control do I have over my health?" Answer: not 100 percent but really quite a bit. Read *How Not to Die* by Michael Greger, MD FACLM, and Gene Stone.[19] It shows that a lot of what people eat causes a lot of diseases.

At your age you probably don't think about your health very much. I didn't when I was your age. You are young and healthy, so you probably don't think that there is anything you need to be concerned about. You would be wrong!

Truth

You can do things now that will destroy your health for the rest of your life and considerably shorten your life. Many of my friends did just that.

Drugs and Alcohol

Randy M., Randy D., Neal, and Scott were my age and close friends when I was in grade school. These guys all used drugs and alcohol in high school.

- Randy M. was one of my best friends in grade school (we rode the same bus), junior high, and high school. He learned to play tennis in my backyard; we were on the high school tennis team together, and he became much better than me! We went to the same college our first year, and he chose to hang out with the "long hairs" (drug users), and I didn't see much of him after that. He was a great athlete and had a great sense of humor. But his older brother Greg died in his early twenties from a drug overdose, and Randy followed his example and became an alcoholic and an addict himself. He died in his midfifties from hepatitis, probably the result of using dirty needles. At his funeral I saw his parents, who had watched both of their children die of self-induced causes. It was terribly sad; I didn't know what to say.

- Neal and Randy D. were my best friends in sixth grade. Both used drugs in high school. Randy was mentally messed up and died in his late fifties. The last time I saw Neal, we were seniors in high school; he was a zombie. He couldn't focus his eyes on me. I don't know if he died, but I would be shocked to learn that he is alive.
- Scott was a good friend at church in fifth and sixth grades. He moved away when we were in seventh grade. The next time I saw him was the summer of 1974 (we were nineteen)—he was a simpleton, just grinning all the time due to drug use. He too was unable to focus his eyes. He got a job taking food trays up the elevator at a hospital where his sister worked. He died in his forties. If you destroy your brain, there is no recovery. It never comes back. A major *fubar!*

All these guys, and millions of other guys and gals I never knew, destroyed their minds and their bodies with drugs and alcohol. It is a horrible tragedy that is *self-induced!* My friends all had promising potential, but all that potential was thrown away for a few moments of drug-induced euphoria. It pains me to remember my lost friends. *What a waste!*

Tobacco Use

I don't know very many people who smoked or used snuff. But the ill effects of tobacco are well documented. One disease brought about by smoking is cancer—a slow and painful death; another is emphysema—a lung disease that prevents your lungs from doing their job, and the sufferer can't breathe. One of my relative's parents were both lifelong (not very long) smokers and both died of emphysema.

Marijuana

Some people will try to tell you that marijuana is not a drug. They are wrong. The drug's name is THC; its chemical composition is $C_{21}H_{30}O_2$. It is becoming legalized in more and more states, so people think that it is not harmful. They are wrong. It is more addictive than cigarettes and alcohol, so once you start, you may not be able to quit. The stupor that it causes is no laughing matter. When used in the long term, your brain will be mush, just like with alcohol and stronger drugs.

Diet

Do not take your health for granted. Your body will only take so much abuse. My friend Tim ate a high-sugar diet for most of his life. About six years ago, he had a stroke, then a year later a heart attack, followed by quadruple bypass surgery. He has diabetes now (which is exploding in the United States and has horrible symptoms). He has lost most of his eyesight and can't drive (only one of the horrible symptoms). He is one year older than me, and we are still good friends (since I was in fifth grade). It pains me to see him suffering. Can you imagine how he thinks about how foolish he was for all those years until his body finally said, "I've had enough!"

The damage that people do to themselves can be irreparable! The symptoms of the damage caused by the abuse are slow to make themselves known, plus they get ignored because who wants to change?! When a person finally accepts that they have symptoms and realizes that they have done damage, it is often too late to go back and undo it: *fubar!*

Exercise

Your body needs regular exercise, or it will deteriorate at a young age. A good friend of mine from church, Dan, died suddenly from a massive heart attack at age fifty-six while he was mowing the yard. He had no prior symptoms…that anyone knew about. (If you ever have a health problem, don't keep it a secret! Get medical help immediately!) Your nanna's father (your great-grandfather) died suddenly from a massive heart attack at age fifty-nine. At the time, your nanna was pregnant with your uncle—her father never knew either of her children. He had been given a stress test to check his heart about six months before he died. It showed nothing wrong (or at least that is what he said). *Daily exercise and a healthy diet, started at an early age, probably would have prevented these health problems and early deaths and the heartache they caused.*

The lesson that I am hoping you will see in all this tragedy is that you need to think about your health. Think about it *now* while you are still young and healthy; start and/or continue practicing good habits, and you may be one of the "lucky" ones who have good health all their lives and die peacefully of old age. So the choices here are:

1. Chase some kind of momentary, feel-good thrill and become addicted; live a short unhappy life full of sickness, broken relationships, regrets, and pain, then die young.
2. OR don't abuse yourself with drugs, alcohol, and tobacco, but don't eat carefully either or exercise regularly; you will have health problems later in life and die young.
3. OR be disciplined in your diet and exercise; have a good chance to live a long, enjoyable life and die peacefully of old age.
   The choice is yours. Make your decision now!

My Story

Diet: I have only recently chosen point number three above after many years of pretty much eating whatever I wanted, though I did run a lot before the steel beam fell on me in 1987. I never got hugely fat—the most I ever weighed was 222 pounds about eight years ago. But my blood pressure was high, and my cholesterol was high, both of which can lead to heart attacks and strokes, both of which are highly debilitating if not fatal. I am taking medication for both issues now. Therefore, I do not have a good track record myself. In the last five years, Margaret and I have tried different diets and are always aware of what we are eating. We have both lost weight but could stand to lose a little more. We are exercising most days. So far nothing disastrous has happened healthwise, but who knows what damage has already been done. Hopefully I have corrected my behavior soon enough.

Drugs, alcohol, and tobacco: I never did drugs at all. It looked like a stupid idea. I did drink alcohol as a young adult, but moderately, and now almost none. (I *really* do not need the calories or the carbs!) I never used tobacco either because it stinks, and it is an obviously bad idea.

Exercise: Since my knee decided it didn't like running anymore about three years ago, I have been riding my bike in the summer and walking most of the rest of the year for an hour a day about five days a week. I do feel better and better, which is something you don't hear very often from people my age. Last August in Rocky Mountain National Park, I felt better than I have since we started going there twenty-one years ago. I climbed Hallett Peak, which I haven't done for years. So that's good, right? I believe that if I keep up the exercise and good eating habits, I have a much better chance of being healthy through old age and dying peacefully without a long illness.

Personally my biggest fear is that I might become disabled by some horrific disease like ALS (aka Lou Gehrig's disease—an autoimmune disease) and become a burden to Margaret or your mom…or you guys! That is a nightmare!

Truth

You have a lot of control over your health. Do what you can to avoid all the mistakes I have outlined above, and then you will have a higher quality of life. *Here's to your health!*

Bonus True Story

My father used to tell me: "You are who you associate with." In other words we tend to take on the characteristics of the people around us. He was advising me to choose my friends carefully. As I was rereading the stories of all the friends in this letter who later ruined their lives with drugs, I realized that, back in the day, I didn't hang out with them any longer when they started to do stupid stuff. Somehow, I think, my father's advice sunk in. These guys were great fun to be with; I loved these guys! *But they were heading in the wrong direction!* I don't remember intentionally eliminating them from my social circle, but I sure did not like the choices they were making, and I knew I didn't want to join them in their drug use. That put distance between us, and eventually I didn't see them anymore. Through the years when I would see some of these guys at a class reunion and see how messed up their brains were, I would wonder, "How did I avoid my former friend's fate?" Was it luck? Was it divine intervention? As I look back from my perspective today, and they are all dead, I believe it was my father's advice: "You are who you associate with."

Look around at your circle of friends. Are they caring about others, or are they selfish? Do they have good hearts? In what direction are they heading? Where would you guess they may be in five to ten years? Is that where you want to be? I hope all your friends pass this test. Since I don't know them, I will leave it to you to decide what is best. Always do your own thinking (letter 4).

As for me, I thank God I did not follow along in my former friends' pathways. And I pray that I have changed my diet and improved my exercise habits in time to avoid a slow and painful disease followed by an early death. Time will tell, but I will try to make the most of whatever life I have left!

With love,
Grandpa

Letter 18: Dating, Marriage, and Sex

Love between a man and a woman can be the most wonderful experience of your life if you do it right. Do it wrong and it will be the greatest tragedy in your life and in the lives of your loved ones (been there, done that).

Dear Eddy and Alan,

The relationship between a man and a woman can be the closest thing on earth that there is to heaven, so let's get it right. Here are my thoughts:

Dating

Ideally dating is the process of looking for a life partner. *Do not* have sex with someone you are dating! See the sex section below. While dating you should be trying to get to know the other person, and you should be sharing your honest self with her. Some people will try to impress the girl and pretend they are someone they are not. Then they wonder why their marriage doesn't work! It's because they negotiated in bad faith. Be honest! (As always.) Let her know you, and hopefully she will respond in kind. Have conversations on subjects that will give you and her insights into the deeper parts of each other's thinking—such as all the subjects I have covered in these letters.

Before asking someone to marry you, have the following conversations *without fail*:

1. *Money*—the most common cause of divorce is money fights. Be partners in finance. Make sure your own financial house is in order. If she is willing to learn, help her learn good financial practices. Before you get engaged, take Financial Peace University *together!* You will find out a lot about each other during the class.

2. *In-laws*—having your in-laws interfere with your marriage is a disaster. Do not marry daddy's little princess, and make sure she is not marrying a momma's boy! When you get married, your parents and her parents should absolutely respect the union between the two of you as more important than the relationship they once had with their children—because their children are not children anymore. They are part of a family of their own.

3. *Church*—differences in faith are hard to work around because a person's faith is deeply important to them. It's a big stumbling block if you don't share the same faith.

4. *Sex*—an important part of marriage (see below).

5. *Children*—how many, and how are you going to raise them? School? Discipline? (Next letter.)

Make sure both of you agree on these potential deal-breakers. It won't guarantee you won't have fights. (In fact, I can guarantee you will have fights!) But these big issues hopefully won't be problematic if you have agreed in advance on them.

Marriage

From letter 3: "Try to plan on not marrying until you are out of school or at least in your last year of college." The reason is that you want to be ready to support yourself and your wife. Getting married is at the point in your life where you are independent from your parents, if you haven't become independent already…and you don't want to be broke while trying to build a marriage.

My experience: I am very well qualified to write a book on how to *not* do marriage. My parents didn't model how to do marriage very well; they fought almost daily, screaming at each other and even getting physically violent sometimes. The other thing they did that did not prepare me well for marriage was spoil me; I was given pretty much everything a kid could want, and I was told I would inherit a huge amount of wealth. I was immature, spoiled, entitled, and in denial of having emotions; I misbehaved and had very low self-respect. Altogether I was a poor candidate for marriage.

When I met your nanna in September 1973, when she and I were both eighteen and freshmen in college, it was amazing to me that someone could like me and want to spend time with me (because I had low self-respect). We seemed to understand each other very well; our minds worked in the same way. We became best friends within weeks and spent time with each other almost every day. I always looked forward to seeing her. Fast forward three-and-a-half years, and we got married in May 1977. I cried. I was so happy because I was going to spend the rest of my life with my best friend.

But there was a fatal flaw…me. I was a spoiled, immature jerk who had some big problems:

1. I didn't know how to do relationships well.
2. I had a *horrible* lack of self-respect as a result of the constant criticism as a child, so my feelings were easily hurt, and that made me mad, and that never ended well.
3. I didn't want to abandon my hermit lifestyle and change who I was.
4. I had been trained to believe that emotions were for the weak—because intellect ruled! So I denied even having emotions.
5. I was just like my parents, and they didn't know how to do marriage either. I was an idiot!

The marriage lasted seventeen years because your nanna was very patient with me, but her patience was eventually exhausted. The day we divorced was the saddest day of my life. You *do not* want to have that experience! And it is especially damaging to your children! Before marriage, please have strong self-respect, a willingness to change, and the heart of a servant toward your spouse-to-be.

True Story

Most people believe that who they are is a product of who their parents taught them to be, the environment in which they were raised, and especially the personality and aptitudes they were born with, which is largely true. But they also believe that they can't change, and I believed *all* of that myself as a young adult. My first wife (your nanna) complained to me about my attitude, that it needed to change, and I replied, "I am who I am. This is who you married. Get used to it!" Look at how stupid that was:

1. I was unwilling to listen to what she had to say. This was horribly disrespectful toward her.
2. It was an act of deliberately closing my mind—as if I already knew it all! *If a person is to learn, they must open their mind.*

3. I was unwilling to believe that there was anything wrong with my behavior—unwilling to believe that the problem could be me. *In life, the problem is always me!*
4. I believed that I could not change, but the truth is that I was unwilling to change.
5. I wanted to remain the spoiled and immature little boy that she had married.

This attitude I had was a big part of why she divorced me. The divorce was easily the most painful experience of my life, which includes having a steel beam fall on me and spending seven weeks in the hospital—in intense pain the whole time. *Avoid divorce if at all possible!*

How to do marriage better, in brief:

- When you are married, ask yourself daily, "How can I serve my spouse?" Ask yourself, "What does love require of me?"
- Margaret and I treat each other as equal partners; neither of us is "the head of the household." On big decisions, we do not do anything unless both of us agree. We each have absolute veto power—the decision is still open for discussion, but we are not moving forward until we both agree on it.
- We have a conversation every week on the same day and time where we can reconnect with each other. Anything either of us wants to talk about is open for discussion. Honest communication is critical—it is a *no-bull* zone! But it's also a safe zone—no criticism!

Make sure that you are both mature adults (not just of adult age) before getting married. Marriage can be a uniting of two humans to the point where there is no longer "I" or "me" but "us." Each of you must be a whole person—none of this "You complete me!" garbage! That is called codependence; you can't be a partner with someone who is not complete and mature.

Sex

Tough subject to write about to the grandsons! But I do have strong feelings about sex that I want to share. The main thing is that there is something very, very special that happens when a man and a woman share that very personal and intimate *expression of love* between them. To have that experience be *unique* with just one person, for your whole life, can cause sex to be a *highly treasured* and meaningful—even sacred—thing between you and your spouse. To consider sex to be a part of dating is a *huge* mistake! To have multiple sex partners over the course of a lifetime means that the uniqueness that can cause sex to be special is gone, and then sex can *never* be special for you: *fubar!* If you engage in casual sex (also known as hooking up), you will have destroyed any chance of having that one and only person in your life with whom you have that very special relationship.

Most of the people in the world have no idea what I am talking about here. Most of the world equates dating to having sex, and it is no more special than going to the restroom—it's just another bodily function. Don't throw away the opportunity to experience how close two people can be—which makes your spouse the most special person in the world. Do not engage in sex until you are married and make sure, as best as you can, that the person you decide to marry is someone you want to spend the rest of your life with. But you do want to talk about sex with a person that you are considering marrying. Make sure that the two of you agree on these points.

Remember the vow I made to myself that was near the end of letter 11? That vow was: "Because I am a man of honor, I will honor my marriage vows and never engage in an extramarital affair." Consider making that vow to your spouse-to-be before you get married.

I know this letter is very brief; all three subjects need more development, but I am not qualified to say much more than I did. Before you attempt to accomplish something this big, get good advice from authors and counselors who are specialists in the field. If you have questions for me, I will be happy to try to give further advice.

Truth

To be "as one" with another person is a wonderful experience. It is as close to heaven as one can get in this life…if you have the right attitude. It is certainly worth your effort to learn how to do it well.

With love,
Grandpa

Letter 19: Raising Children

Parenting is a huge responsibility; it requires extreme thought and care.

Dear Alan and Eddy,

This letter will require you to imagine yourself as a parent. But maybe that won't be too hard, because I remember that when I was a kid and didn't like something my parents did to me, I would think, "I sure won't do *that* to my kids!" And I didn't. But there was still *a lot* that I would have done differently as a father if I had known better. In this letter I will attempt to teach you guys what I have learned. It could be a much longer letter because it's a big subject. So look for other resources and learn as much as you can before having children.

As a parent you should help your children understand the objective of life.

Children believe that pleasing themselves should be what life is all about. They are wrong; becoming better people should be their goal. All children should be taught (from letter 2): "Who you are is your responsibility!" It is your responsibility to change yourself into a loving, compassionate human. This is the sixth time (at least) you have seen this, but it bears repeating from a parental perspective. As a good parent, it should be your goal to teach your children to be better and better every day—to be more responsible, more mature, more loving, to become adults so that when they are old enough...*they will move out! Ha ha!* But seriously, if you want your children to have a *good life*, teach them to be *good people. If you love them, teach them to be loving.*

I have known parents whose goal as a parent was to do anything they could to make the life of their children as nice and as easy as they could make it—to spare them from any grief or pain. In doing this, all they accomplished was to prepare their children to be lifelong children—and be lifelong unhappy. They didn't allow the child to learn how to deal with hardship, so their child remained immature and irresponsible. To some degree my own parents did this to me. What they should have done is to prepare me to be an adult, especially teaching me to expect to *earn* everything I get.

As a parent you are a teacher. Here's how *not* to do it. As I said in the self-respect letter (letter 7), "my parents were emotionally distant from us kids: never a hug, never a 'good job' or a 'well done,' never an 'I love you.' But always an endless stream of criticism, yelling, and hitting." I was taught to deny having emotions and to be rigid in my thinking—that is, believing that I had all the answers and being unwilling to listen to anyone else's opinion. This is the exact opposite of who you want to be as a spouse or a parent...as a person!

How to Do It Better:

- First and foremost, be loving and affectionate with your children. Let there be no doubt in their minds that they are loved!
- Be a good listener, but don't be too sympathetic because in every problem there is always a lesson. So listen to everything the child wants to say, and when the child has said all there is to say, ask your child what they think they should do. This will engage their minds and give them the *responsibility* for finding a solution. Then listen again, and give gentle advice and lessons.
- Explain carefully why your advice is the best way to handle the situation and why you would not advise the other options. Teach them how to think critically, to look at the probable outcomes of various options, and thereby, make better decisions.
- Make your home a safe place for your children. Never allow violence, criticism, or condemnation.
- Make your home a place of order. There must be expectations of behavior (rules), consequences for violating the rules that are made clear in advance, and enforcement of the consequences in a fair and consistent manner.
- The rights of all members of the family, and people outside the family, must be honored and protected. That's why we have rules of behavior—to protect the rights of others. This needs to be taught and demonstrated always!
- Please, please let your child deal with life's challenges to the extent that they are able. As your children learn to deal with small problems, let them deal with larger and larger problems with you teaching lessons along the way. This is the path to adulthood. Please do not be a "helicopter parent!" I feel sorry for those kids because their life is going to be *hell!* They will not

know how to think critically, make decisions, and deal with issues. They will be immature and incapable.

When you are with your child *be fully present!*

Instead of plugging your child into an electronic babysitter by giving them a video screen of some kind for entertainment, talk to them. Make it a habit to take your child for a walk outside and enjoy a little exercise, and while outside have a conversation about what you are observing in the world. While walking and talking, you are developing in the child a curiosity about the world. You will develop their minds while they develop their bodies and create good habits.

Minimize your use of electronic devices when you are with your child—*be fully present!* I have seen families together at a restaurant, and both parents and all children have an electronic device upon which each of them is totally focused. Here is an opportunity for the family to have a conversation and bond...and they're ignoring each other! What a loss!

That is why the art of conversation is becoming a lost art. Do what you can to develop in your children the ability to talk to people—they must listen carefully and respond. How can they develop relationships otherwise? Face-to-face communication, if possible, is always the best.

What You Want to Teach and Model with Your Life:

- First, they need to know that their life is theirs to do with as they wish (letter 1), but while they are still dependent on you, you are in charge of them. When they reach adulthood, no one can live their life for them. This is a great freedom, which is exciting, but it is also a great responsibility (letter 2). *They must be told early and often that as adults they must provide for their own welfare (happiness, well-being, and day-to-day necessities).*

- See life as a great adventure made up of many experiments of various sizes—some big, some small: "Let's try this and see what happens." Experiment within reason; don't be foolish!

- Have wide-eyed curiosity about the world and other people and what makes life worth all the trouble. (Because it certainly is worth it!) *Be a lifelong learner!*

- Teach them to be loving and considerate of other people but not to cater to their wrongful thinking. Teach your children that if they see a friend going in the wrong direction, they should tell the friend so and not support or go along with the friend in their mistake.

- Teach your children the lessons I have learned in my life and have written to you in these letters…if you agree with them and practice them.

- Above all, do not try to teach something that you yourselves are not living out in your lives. That is called being hypocritical; it is dishonest, and your children will see right through you, and you will have no authority over them.

Discipline

Speaking of having authority, while you want to be reasonable and lead with gentleness, *as parents, you and your spouse are absolutely in charge of the family.* You will have more experience, and if you have learned from that experience, you will be wiser than your children. Also if you are paying the bills, you have the say so. That is your right. And legally, as far as I know, you are responsible for the actions of your children until they reach the legal age (eighteen in most states), so that gives the parent legal authority as well.

Do not let your children be in charge. They don't know what they are doing! Your household will be upside down, and your children will *suffer* because of it. Without learning discipline and self-control, they will feed every selfish notion that comes into their heads, and they will be miserable in adulthood when they reach that age, because their parents didn't teach them to be disciplined, and their life will be out of control. Also children *want* to know what to do and how to manage life. Please give them what they need and what they want: discipline, learning, and love.

How to administer discipline: with firmness but not with violence. Take away privileges and freedoms for a time, the length of which should be in proportion to the offense. Be consistent and reasonable; make sure that the child knows why the discipline is being given. Do it in agreement and with the support of your spouse—something that needs to be discussed with your spouse before you get married (letter 18). Do it with love because it is for the good of the child.

I wish this is how I had raised my children. What I did as a parent was the best I could do with what I knew at the time, but I was ignorant. So please be wise and learn from me *and others* so that you will know better! The responsibility of parenting is *big* because the attitudes your children approach life with will be the attitudes you modeled and taught. Approach parenting with care and lots of learning for yourself.

My family has brought me great joy. And having you guys in my life is a big part of that joy. So look forward to parenting…but not until you are ready! That is, being financially stable and married.

There is a whole lot more, of course, but when I became a parent at twenty-five, I didn't know this much. The main thing is, your job as a parent is to guide your children to become adults through example, loving instruction, and discipline. *Make sure that you and your spouse are together on this.* Otherwise, your children will learn nothing from you except how to play the two of you against each other. Get a book that is highly recommended. Sorry, I do not know of one.

With love,
Grandpa

Letter 20: Halftime

If you are smart with money, you will be able to retire early, then use the rest of your life to be passionate about service to others! What a joy!

Dear Eddy and Alan,

*T*his is where life gets *very* exciting and *very* rewarding! This is where we take letter 16—"Be In-Service to Others"—and make it a big part of your plan for your life (if you want to). This letter looks at the latter part of life—the part that is after "halftime." This idea of halftime came from Bob Buford who wrote a book with that title. We liked the book so much we bought a case of *Halftime*[20] books and taught a class at church on it. We still have three unused books left; if you want one let me know.

Buford's idea[20] is this: Imagine you are a young adult, married with children. At that time you are mainly concerned with paying the bills and raising the kids, and rightly so. But as the years pass, and you build financial stability, then wealth, and then the kids grow up and move out, you might start to think, *"What have I really accomplished?"* You might start to wonder if there is more to life than just taking care of yourself and your family. Hopefully you will start thinking these thoughts before then...like now, maybe. Taking care of yourself and your family is certainly important and should be given first priority in your finances. But at some point, if you work hard enough and save hard enough, long enough, you become financially independent. Financial independence comes when you have built enough wealth that you no longer have to earn a living because your investments are earning enough income to pay all your living expenses.

At the time you have reached financial independence, you will be able to retire. This isn't a specific date or age; you can reach financial independence sooner than the forty-plus years of work most people take, or much sooner than age sixty-five if you save more and spend less. Margaret and I will have accomplished going from broke to financial independence in about nineteen years, three years from now. The sooner you start and the harder you work and save, the sooner you will get there. Without having to work for a living, you no longer must spend forty or more hours a week at your job, or in your business if you own one, and you can spend that time doing something else. This is what the book calls "halftime." It is a time to pause, reflect, and decide what to do with the rest of your life. Actually you can start thinking about this before you are ready to retire. You can start thinking about what to do with the rest of your life *now!*

There is another possibility: you could choose, as a career or business, something that serves your fellow mankind and let your career or business provide your income as you build wealth for retirement. A great example of this is Dave Ramsey. He started out in his business of helping people with financial issues as a sideline while he earned an income as a real estate agent. It turned out that there was a huge need for the advice he offered, and his system of Baby Steps really worked! (Just ask us!) Last I heard, he built that business of service into a good-sized enterprise, employing nearly a thousand people. His books and classes have helped millions, and his professional handling of his business made him very wealthy at the same time. It's the best of both worlds. So you too might consider a career or business of service to earn a living and build wealth for retirement.

Most people use retirement as a time of self-indulgence. Some like to fish; some like to play golf; some like to travel. Whatever you enjoy is fine for a vacation, but where is the joy in serving yourself all the time? I tried serving myself for many years, as I described in letter 15, and it is no fun, and I was not happy—not fulfilled.

True Story

I know a woman who retired a few years ago. She and her husband bought a house in Florida near the gulf coast where they spend their winters. They recently bought a new house here in town, of about three thousand square feet (twice the size of our house) on three acres where they have installed a new swimming pool, and they are completely remodeling the inside. They just got back from a four- or five-week trip to Europe and are heading to Florida for the winter soon. Sounds great, doesn't it? But I wouldn't trade places with her for anything.

Why is she, living in the lap of luxury, not to be envied? Because serving oneself is a dead end. There is no long-term satisfaction to it. It is called hedonism—"the doctrine that pleasure or happiness is the sole or chief good in life".[21] It is futile—"serving no useful purpose".[22] Here's what happens: we get bored, change the scenery, get bored, spend money on ourselves, get bored, change the scenery again...and wonder why we're so bored. I believe that we crave to have purpose. As long as we have goals that we are striving to attain, we have a reason to get up in the morning. But if our only goal is to entertain ourselves, it gets boring quickly.

This is where letter 16 comes into play. Service to others is a great thing to do as a part-time volunteer when you are young and still in school or working for a living, and it is a great thing to teach and model for your children, but if upon retirement it is pursued as a full-time occupation, it could bring untold joy to your life. To help people who need help is an awesome feeling; to do it all the time would be incredible. This is where we want to be soon. Does that make sense? Margaret and I will find out soon, and I will let you guys know.

Take this wisdom and make it a part of your whole life from now until the day you die, and then you will die as "the luckiest man on the face of this earth," as Lou Gehrig,[23] the famous baseball player, called himself. Read his short speech delivered on July 4, 1939. It's available on the internet. He had been recently diagnosed with the (still) incurable disease ALS (amyotrophic lateral sclerosis), also known as Lou Gehrig's disease. Lou Gehrig played for the New York Yankees and, at various times in his career, played with Babe Ruth and Joe DiMaggio. He had been given a deadly diagnosis, had come to accept the imminent end of his life, and gave a speech of gratitude for the wonderful blessings he had enjoyed in his life. The speech has been an inspiration for uncountable millions of people since 1939, and now for you guys if you haven't read it before. It brings tears to my eyes every time I read it or hear it, but don't let that be a cause for you to not read it. Just keep a box of tissues handy.

The next letter I will send you is about death, and it would be great if I have that much gratitude in my heart at the time of my death, so this is kind of a segue to the next letter.

Be in Service to Others—this is the biggest secret and the greatest joy in life! If you make it a part of your life, for your whole life, the joy and gratitude you experience will be greater than you can imagine!

With love,
Grandpa

Letter 21: Death

It is a part of life.

Dear Alan and Eddy,

You are probably wondering why a letter about death. Isn't that morbid and depressing? I would ask, "Is it?" It is only morbid and depressing if you fear it. Since I have been very close to death once, I probably have more experience than 98 percent of people on the subject, and I am not in the least afraid of death. So as it turns out, your grandpa may be very well qualified to speak on this subject. I would like to share my experience with you, and hopefully, it will then not be a subject to avoid and fear, but instead, as stated above, it is a part of life. "No one is getting out of this alive," I have heard Dave Ramsey say. (I don't remember where.)

True Story

My close encounter with death happened on August 15, 1987, when I had a steel beam fall on me. We have covered parts of that experience and some of the lessons that I learned on that day and in the weeks after. In letter 8, I wrote that when I realized that the beam was falling, "three thoughts came into my mind: 'Oh, shit! I'm dead. I'm glad I have good life insurance.' I remember thinking those three thoughts very clearly as if it was yesterday." In that letter, I wrote about a vision I had that happened in an instant. After that vision I was given a choice to live or die. I was given knowledge that either choice was "OK," and that to die meant I would go somewhere that was much more preferable than planet Earth. I thought of my wife, your nanna, and I knew that she would be OK without me—it would be tough, but she was a strong and determined person. Plus, she would have financial stability because we had life insurance, our house was paid off, and we didn't have much debt. So…I decided to die! Then I thought of my children; your uncle was seven and your mom was four. I felt they were too young to be without their father, so I changed my mind and decided to fight it out…and live. The doctors told your nanna that I would not live past the night of the accident. The next morning, they told her that I was somehow still alive but would not last another twenty-four hours; the morning after that, they said the same thing again! Three times they promised her that I was surely going to die, but I didn't die. I survived. I am glad I did survive because I would not have known you guys if I had not! And I would not be able to share these letters with you.

Why did I survive? The doctors had no explanation. All my ribs were broken, my left lung had collapsed (the lung cavity was full of blood, so my lung could not expand), and my right lung was simply full of blood. They attempted to measure my lung capacity, and

I couldn't budge the needle—my lung capacity was officially zero! I survived on tiny sips of air because trying to breathe was excruciating. One good thing was my lungs were very healthy prior to the accident because I was a runner at the time. But the main reason I survived was because I knew I could. I had been given a choice to live or die, so both were possibilities. I had made my decision to live, and that was that! It was a case of mind over matter.

But don't forget that I first chose to die. It was the easiest choice because I knew that my wife would be OK, and I knew I would go somewhere far better than earth because I had been given that sure knowledge. I have never been afraid to die since that day.

So I have no fear of death because I know that death is not the end of me. That was given to me by the vision and by the knowledge that there was a better place for me to be.

So how is that an advantage? I have a bigger picture of life than most people. I am not all caught up in the soap opera issues most people fill their idle hours with. (Soap opera is a slang term from my youth; I don't know if it is still used. It refers to daytime television shows that had high drama and were sponsored by soap companies because the audience was mainly housewives. Is the term "housewife" even used anymore?) Most people get disturbed by others' illnesses or death (or their own), or whatever tragedy might strike. And there is no shortage of tragedy out there—I have experienced a bucketload of it myself. Tragedy is real; I wrote about it in letters 9 and 10. When I can, I try to help because I know it is painful and devastating for the person upon whom it strikes. But I also know that life on earth is temporary, and if things look grave, I think to myself, "This too shall pass." I have sure knowledge that, even if complete disaster comes, it will be OK. "Healing will come in this life…or the next," my good friend Donna Hoover once said. RIP.

I wish I could pass that peaceful assurance on to you guys—this letter is my attempt to do that. My hope is that you will read carefully all that I have written in these letters...and read them again and again. If you try some of my ideas, find that they work, and apply the lessons to your life, you will experience a better quality of life. Then you will also discover Truths of your own. And after a while, you will find a life of peace in harmony with natural law; you will come to know that there is a bigger picture out there that is far bigger than this world. And you too will have that peaceful assurance of "This too shall pass." This idea is also referenced in my final letter (23—just two more after this one!).

So life is temporary. Make the most of it! Learn all you can, be a person you can be proud of, work hard and smart, have great relationships, and have lots of joy! Do not let the shadow of death spoil it! Because death won't spoil it—you have my promise!

With love,
Grandpa

Letter 22: What's It All About?

What is the purpose in life?

Dear Eddy and Alan,

We are getting near the end of the letters—just one more after this one. My purpose in writing these letters is simple: the one thing I hope for most, after writing all these letters of true stories and advice, is that you guys will try at least some of these Truths. Test them to see if you get a good result. If the result is truly good, you will want to apply it to your life going forward. Keep testing your beliefs for a better and better life. Discover Truths of your own and test them, always looking for a better way. The sooner you get started, the sooner you will start getting results, and you will go further than me because I got a late start—at forty-three years of age. For you guys, the sky's the limit! Enjoy your life as much as you can as soon as you can. I can tell you… *I sure wish I had started learning this stuff at your age!* I wasted a lot of years and caused myself and my family an incredible amount of grief, pain, and regret because I pursued stupid, selfish desires. I hope that from reading my True Stories you can see this is true. If you live out the Truths contained in these letters, you will have a far better life than me. I hope, like anything, that will be the case.

If you follow the advice in these letters, you will have a good life:

1. By taking responsibility for your life, you gain freedom and empowerment.
2. By thinking independently, you are self-directed and not following the crowd.
3. By using critical thinking, you can discern Truth, make better decisions, and not be misled.
4. By being honest and hardworking, you gain self-respect...and a livelihood.
5. By managing money well, you gain financial stability and wealth.
6. By serving others, you experience joy.
7. By giving generously, you become a generous person.
8. By sharing love with others, you gain good relationships and have fun.
9. By exercising and eating the right foods, you gain good health and feel good.
10. By having a lifelong commitment through marriage, you have a family, which gives you a purpose bigger than yourself.

All the above would add up to a good life, wouldn't you agree? This is a very short question, but do not miss the gigantic importance of its answer. Think about it for a while. Wouldn't it be great to have a life that included all the above? And more? Because this is not a complete list!

A good life. If you follow my advice, a good life is yours, starting *now*!

What about a great life? What would a great life look like? A great life would be a life with lasting purpose. We talked about goals: create a goal, make a plan to attain the goal, and work the plan. This is how to accomplish what you want in life.

Your goals give you direction; a life of purpose is different. It is long term—longer than your life! Sometimes people talk about leaving a legacy, something that is valuable to others after you have passed on. Purpose is longer lasting than even that.

What is the purpose in life?

If there is no life beyond our time here on earth, then all our work and effort for self-improvement ends with our death, and eventually, everything we created with our life crumbles to dust. Everything humans create is temporary. Some man-made things have lasted thousands of years; the pyramids in Egypt and the Great Wall of China are two examples. But even these, without constant maintenance, will turn to dust someday. So everything you or I create on earth only lasts for a period of time, so our perspective of life will be tainted with the ultimate reality that we are nothing more significant than ants working on an anthill. Think about it.

In 1987 I got a glimpse of a longer-lasting purpose in life when I experienced seeing my life flash before my eyes, as I related to you in letter 8. That vision caused me to conclude that *love is the only thing we will take with us when we leave this earth.*

Part of the message of that vision is that there is an afterlife. In my letter before this one, I wrote: "My hope is that you will read carefully all that I have written in these letters…you will find a life of peace in harmony with natural law; you will come to know that there is a bigger picture out there that is far bigger than this world." So I am talking about the afterlife, a bigger perspective than just this world. I am talking about God and the ultimate purpose of human life.

Except for a few times in a slight way while writing these letters, I have intentionally left out the one thing that I believe truly unifies all Truths…and is in fact the source of Truth. The reason I left out the biggest part of my belief system of what life is about is this: I wanted to argue for my beliefs from a purely logical and practical perspective. I want you guys to see Truth without anything getting in the way. I hope I have done that. I hope you can learn from my experience, apply these lessons to your lives, and have a far better life than I had (before now—now I'm having fun and loving it!). If you learn and apply to your lives these lessons in the letters, then my effort in writing all these letters will have been well worth it.

All the Truth, as far as I understand it, points to this letter and its Truth: *God is the reason for our existence, the creator of our world and universe and us, and the source of all Reason, Truth, Logic, and Love.* Because God laid down the laws of the universe before He created the universe, the Truth is perfectly practical, perfectly logical, perfectly integrated, and perfectly complete. It controls everything in the universe except us because we have free will; we get to choose how we believe and behave, and as you know, this gives us ultimate responsibility for the outcome of our lives. Since God created the universe and placed us on earth, Truth is perfectly practical. Therefore, if we discover these Truths and choose to live our lives in accordance with them, our lives will *automatically* be blessed because our lives will be in harmony with the universe and with God. But if we choose to pursue our selfish desires, our lives will be a mess, and the outcome of our lives will be tragedy. So *please* do not throw away all the Truth contained in these letters just because you may not like the contents of this letter. The blessings of living your life in harmony with Truth will certainly still be yours to enjoy no matter how you feel about or whether you believe in the existence of God. That being said, I would like to lay down my reasons for my belief that God exists and is the creator of the universe and all of us humans.

My reasons for believing that God exists are in four parts:

1. My personal experiences of God: This is, for me, the most immediate and undeniable certainty of God's existence. Some of my experiences are in these letters. For other people, my experiences are not as convincing, I'm sure, because they didn't happen to them. But they did happen to me, so unless you believe that I am crazy or a liar, they must provide some credence.

2. My logical reason for God's existence: Natural laws exist; science has proven that. But where did those laws come from? Who created them? They had to be in existence before creation so that creation could happen. They must continue to be in force and effect in order for creation to continue to exist. The study of nature (science) is the study of God's laws, and it gives one an understanding of who God is if the scientist has an open mind.

3. My suppositions as to the reason for creation and the purpose of life and how they support points one and two above: the goal in life, as I have stated many times in these letters, is for us to change ourselves from perfectly selfish into perfectly loving souls, for the purpose of becoming mature and loving enough to have a personal relationship with God.

4. The fact that living these Truths in these letters *does* make for a better life, and the fact that these Truths also agree with almost all the lessons taught by Jesus in the Bible. All Truth is practical, united,

consistent, flawless, and simple. When things get "complicated," that is manmade and is not Truth. (Some of these complications are in the Bible and in *all* religions, so a person must practice discernment [letter 5] at all times!)

Where Does Religion Come In?

Religion and God are two very separate and often different things. *God is a spiritual being* who is the perfect Creative Intelligence behind the creation of the universe, as well as the Creator of you and me. To a great degree, He is a mystery, but He is not unknowable. I have been seeking God and growing my knowledge of Him through understanding his creation—a learning environment that reflects its creator—and how life works. However, the Truth is hidden (letter 5). We must seek Truth in order to find it.

Religion is manmade. At its best, it is an attempt to help people find God, but *no* religion is perfect. At its worst, it can be a tangle of nonsensical beliefs that cause people to reject God. I go to church and tithe and volunteer, but I do not hold membership because I will never subordinate my thinking to someone else who wants to tell me what to believe. I go to a church that follows Jesus and teaches the lessons Jesus taught (not easy to find). I follow Jesus because almost all of what he is quoted as saying is True, because I have tested it and continue to test it by living out those lessons that work. What does not work is not true, and I cannot apply those lessons to my life, so I do not claim to believe them...and set them aside.

One Final Proof of God—A True Story

At a family reunion about fifteen years ago, a group of my cousins was taking a hike with Margaret and me. Suddenly without any preamble, my cousin, who is an outspoken atheist, said to me, "Mike, prove to me that God exists!" I was slightly stunned and totally unprepared for such a challenge. I am the youngest cousin, and he is a lot older, far smarter, and has much more credibility than I do. Plus, I had never attempted to prove that God existed and had no idea what to say for a moment.

Then out of nowhere, I heard my mouth say these words: "Do you believe in love?" The thought was not mine, but I knew that his wife was right in front of him and would easily hear all that was said. My cousin had been married to her for about thirty years at that time, and they had two adult daughters and another nearly adult daughter, all of whom he loved very much. I also realized that the debate had reached checkmate with one question!

He was in a corner with no escape. He had to say, "Yes," which he did, rather sheepishly, because he too realized that he was in a corner. I said, again not my words, "Explain to me what love is in a world devoid of spirit." He couldn't answer...and has not answered to this day. I can't find any defense for atheism in this debate either. By the way, the man has a brilliant mind, with a doctorate in mathematics; but he was arguing with a superior intellect—the inventor of Truth. My cousin thought he was debating me, but he was debating God, and God won! I don't know if that short conversation caused him to modify his belief in atheism or not, but it is to me a hands-down winner!

This is a *very brief* overview of a subject that is infinite in its nature.

I have exposed a small bit of my understanding of God and the purpose of life. It would take a book to do the subject justice. In fact I already have the outline of the book written. I started that book before your mom asked me to write these letters. I hope I live long enough to finish it. I also hope that there is enough here to arouse your interest. I would love to continue our conversation anytime.

The bottom line as I stated in letter 1: "Your life is yours to do with as you wish." This is so True. It is your choice to believe or not believe what I have written here—any of it! But before you throw it out, think about it and test it, just one little part of it.

With love,
Grandpa

Letter 23: A Bright Future!

It's up to you!

Dear Alan and Eddy,

This is the last letter! That may make you sad, or it may make you relieved. But it had to come to an end sometime, right? It has been my great joy to write these letters to you guys. I have been tremendously blessed in trying to write my philosophy in a coherent, unified, and logical way. And I tried to make it practical at the same time so that you could apply it to your lives. I hope and pray that you have enjoyed the letters, that they have been understood and meaningful to you guys, and that you will keep them and refer to them in the future. I hope that these letters are a blessing to you.

You guys have a beautiful, bright future! You are lucky to be where you are: planning your life with the entire horizon, all 360 degrees of direction to choose from. You also have something I didn't have: a lot of lessons—learned (by me and others) the hard way—that you can learn from without having to learn them through trial and error and pain! You have a great head start...if you choose to use it.

I would like to end these twenty-three letters with someone else's writing. It is a poem by Rudyard Kipling. This poem captures my feelings toward you guys very well. It is an expression of hope for a great future for a younger generation—it is my hope for you guys.

With love,
Grandpa

If

By Rudyard Kipling

If you can keep your head when all about you
Are losing theirs and blaming it on you;
If you can trust yourself when all men doubt you,
But make allowance for their doubting too:
If you can wait and not be tired by waiting,
Or, being lied about, don't deal in lies,
Or being hated don't give way to hating,
And yet don't look too good, nor talk too wise;

If you can dream—and not make dreams your master;
If you can think—and not make thoughts your aim,
If you can meet with Triumph and Disaster
And treat those two impostors just the same:
If you can bear to hear the truth you've spoken
Twisted by knaves to make a trap for fools,
Or watch the things you gave your life to, broken,
And stoop and build 'em up with worn-out tools;

If you can make one heap of all your winnings
And risk it on one turn of pitch-and-toss,
And lose, and start again at your beginnings,
And never breathe a word about your loss:
If you can force your heart and nerve and sinew
To serve your turn long after they are gone,
And so hold on when there is nothing in you
Except the Will which says to them: "Hold on!"

If you can talk with crowds and keep your virtue,
Or walk with Kings—nor lose the common touch,
If neither foes nor loving friends can hurt you,
If all men count with you, but none too much:
If you can fill the unforgiving minute
With sixty seconds' worth of distance run,
Yours is the Earth and everything that's in it,
And—which is more—you'll be a Man, my son! [24]

Bibliography

1. Warshaw, Jade. "How to Stop Living Paycheck to Paycheck." *Ramsey Solutions*, July 20, 2023. https://www.ramseysolutions.com/budgeting/stop-living-paycheck-to-paycheck.
2. ONeal, Anthony. *Debt-Free Degree*. Ramsey Press, 2019
3. Hazlitt, Henry. (1979). *Economics in One Lesson: The Shortest & Surest Way to Understand Basic Economics*. Currency. This idea is developed from p. 17.
4. *Merriam-Webster.com Dictionary*, s.v. "utopia," accessed August 5, 2023, https://www.merriam-webster.com/dictionary/utopia.
5. Ramsey, D. (2022). *Baby Steps Millionaires: How ordinary people built extraordinary wealth-and how you can too*. Ramsey Press, The Lampo Group, LLC.
6. World Health Organization. *COVID-19 pandemic triggers 25% increase in prevalence of anxiety and depression worldwide*. https://www.who.int/news/item/02-03-2022-covid-19-pandemic-triggers-25-increase-in-prevalence-of-anxiety-and-depression-worldwide. Accessed August 15, 2023.
7. Carnegie, Dale. (1984). *How to Stop Worrying and Start Living*. Pocket Books.
8. https://en.wikipedia.org/wiki/What_does_not_kill_me_makes_me_stronger. Accessed 5 Aug. 2023.
9. *Merriam-Webster.com Dictionary*, s.v. "adult," accessed August 5, 2023, https://www.merriam-webster.com/dictionary/adult.
10. *Merriam-Webster.com Dictionary*, s.v. "mature," accessed August 5, 2023, https://www.merriam-webster.com/dictionary/mature.
11. Al-Anon. *The Twelve Steps*. https://al-anon.org/for-members/the-legacies/the-twelve-steps/. Accessed August 15, 2023.

12. Smith System website: https://www.drivedifferent.com accessed August 5, 2023.

13. Smith System, 94% of crashes involve driver error: accessed August 5, 2023. https://www.drivedifferent.com/deaths-traffic-accidents-rise/

14. Ramsey, Dave. (2013). *The Total Money Makeover.* Thomas Nelson.

15. Ramsey, Dave, quote. https://undefeatedmotivation.com/quotes/live-like-no-else-today-so-you-can-live-like-no-else-tomorrow-dave-ramsey-quote/. Accessed August 16, 2023.

16. Ramsey Solutions. "…giving is the most fun you can have with money!" accessed August 5, 2023. https://www.ramseysolutions.com/budgeting/giving-is-the-most-rewarding.

17. Lupton, Robert D. (2012) *Toxic charity: How churches and charities hurt those they help (and how to reverse it).* New York: HarperOne.

18. Lupton, Robert D. (2016) *Charity Detox: What Charity Would Look Like If We Cared About Results.* New York: HarperOne.

19. Greger, Michael MD FACLM, and Gene Stone. (2015) *How Not to Die.* Flatiron Books.

20. Buford, Bob. (1994) *Halftime.* Zondervan.

21. "Hedonism." Merriam-Webster.com Dictionary, Merriam-Webster, https://www.merriam-webster.com/dictionary/hedonism. Accessed 6 Jun. 2023.

22. "Futile." Merriam-Webster.com Dictionary, Merriam-Webster, https://www.merriam-webster.com/dictionary/futile. Accessed 6 Jun. 2023.

23. Gehrig, Lou, "the luckiest man on the face of this earth". Accessed August 6, 2023. https://baseballhall.org/discover-more/stories/baseball-history/lou-gehrig-luckiest-man.

24. Kipling, Rudyard. If. https://www.familyfriendpoems.com/poem/if-by-rudyard-kipling.

Acknowledgements

To my daughter, thank you for a great idea! Hope you like the result.

To my wife, thank you for your encouragement and support. I couldn't have done it without you!

To God, I pray this helps.

About the Author

I was born in 1955 in Missouri, and have lived in Missouri my whole life, except for a brief stint at the University of Kansas in Lawrence. Married to my first wife of 18 years, with two children. Married to my second wife 22 years – trying to do it better this time!

From 1980 through 1992 I was a house builder and real estate developer, started driving a semi-truck in 1993 when I went broke. Drove a truck for about 22 years off and on, now retired. Truck driving gave me a lot of time alone, and I used that time to think. My failures in business and marriage were the first subjects to work through, then I moved on to, "What IS the meaning of life anyway?" I am still working through that subject. Stay tuned!